CATHY CROSHAW   a memoir

The BREAST DEFENSE *Is a* GD OFFENSE

Facing Life and Breast Cancer with
an Infusion of Humor and Attitude

RIVER GROVE
BOOKS

The names and identifying characteristics of persons referenced in this book have been changed to protect their privacy. While the persons and conversations portrayed in the book are based on actual events, some of the direct quotes and dialogue are a product of the author's imagination.

Published by River Grove Books
Austin, TX
www.rivergrovebooks.com

Distributed by River Grove Books

Design and composition by Greenleaf Book Group
Cover design by Greenleaf Book Group
Cover images used under license from @Shutterstock.com/Millisentaww

Publisher's Cataloging-in-Publication data is available.

Print ISBN: 978-1-63299-281-9

eBook ISBN: 978-1-63299-282-6

First Edition

To the staff of the Gene Upshaw Memorial Tahoe Forest Cancer Center. Thank you all for your kindness, compassion, and professionalism.

"The good thing about cancer (and yes, there are good things) is the way it helps you prioritize your life. You learn what is important—love, family, friends, being nice to the other people we share this earth with, being nice to the earth, too. That's the lesson—to live that way without having to go through the pain. My friend Gilda Radner put it this way: 'If it weren't for the downside, everybody would want to have cancer. But there is a heck of a downside.'"

—Joel Siegel

CONTENTS

WHY I WROTE *This* BOOK

I HAD NO GOALS WHATSOEVER when I began writing this book. In fact, I had no intention of writing a book at all. One evening, however, I was on a business trip and alone in a hotel room in the San Francisco Bay Area. I couldn't get the TV to work. I have no patience for electronics that do not respond immediately to my coaxing. I was in my jammies, all tucked into bed, and definitely didn't feel like calling the front desk and having the guy come to my room to help me with the TV. Faced with the intransigent TV, I picked up my laptop, and a few pages of something related to my cancer experience simply poured out of me.

When I read what I'd written the next morning, my first impression was one of dreamlike disconnection, as if I were floating above myself, observing an experience I had not connected with as it unfolded. I showed what I had written to my husband, Bob, who encouraged me to continue. Then I sent it to my sister, Laura, who loved it and offered to be a co-author from the family's perspective. We even went so far as to plan what we would wear on *Oprah*. Finally, I sent it to my mom, who cried. Soon after, I was off and running.

Six Things

From that sketchy beginning, a manuscript unfolded. Along the way, some clear goals emerged from the rubble of my words. These goals inspired me to devote hours, days, and weeks to this endeavor. As I discovered in writing this book, I hope to accomplish six things. If I can do that, I'll be happy with my efforts. Here are the items that made my list:

1. **Make one person smile when they least expect it.** Cancer is not a topic that evokes smiles; it's quite the opposite actually. But there can be funny moments or circumstances that lift your spirits and help you through the ordeal. If I can capture just a few of those moments and make you laugh or smile in the midst of a difficult day, I will have accomplished the most important item on my list. But be aware that not all of the book directly relates to my cancer experience. Cancer, in my case (and as I suspect it is in many cases), was a culmination of events and lifestyle choices, some of which you may relate to and some of which you may not. But you may also find some humor in the backstory—I know I have. Frankly, if you haven't found any humor in your life so far, I offer you mine.

2. **Provide a hopeful and positive perspective on what to expect if you are facing a cancer diagnosis.** I suspect that many people who have not experienced cancer are unaware of the details of the diagnosis and treatment process. I was in this camp when I was first diagnosed, and it was pretty scary. Even if you are more informed than I was, you may not appreciate what it feels like to live through the experience. In sharing my story, I hope to provide a picture of what to expect and thereby allay some of your fears or concerns.

3. **Share some resources that can help you through your treatment.** I was often pleasantly surprised at the many perks available to cancer patients. I want you to know right now that there is a ton of information out there (online, at your doctor's office, and at treatment centers) and countless services to help you through the experience emotionally, financially and physically. I expected that counseling and possibly nutritional advice might be available to me at the cancer center, but I had no idea that there would also be massages, yoga classes, cooking classes for patients and caregivers, and cosmetology sessions. These are only a few of the services offered by either the local cancer center, the American Cancer Society, or other organizations.

   Frankly, these resources and benefits are usually offered at a time when you are already overwhelmed, because you have just been told that you have cancer. I know that I never read the handouts I got from the cancer center until I started writing this book. I was actually stunned to find out that a lot of the perks that I stumbled upon when going through my treatment were listed right there.

   I hope you will be more receptive to absorbing the available benefits than I was. If not, perhaps my personal narrative will help you. Given the flood of breast-cancer information available on the Internet, I don't recommend that as a starting point. It's not that I have anything against online searches. Once you know what's out there, you'll be able to seek out the things that make sense for you. You could start with this book and branch out from there.

4. **Help others understand the patient's perspective.** I tend to go through life tremendously concerned about saying the wrong thing to someone in a crisis. Consequently, I usually

say the wrong thing. Nevertheless, I am hopeful that sharing my experience can help someone close to you—or even a stranger—to say or do the right thing when you need it most.

5. **Do a good deed.** I plan to donate a portion of any profits from this book to the American Cancer Society and the "cancer spa," as I came to know the Gene Upshaw Memorial Tahoe Forest Cancer Center, to help those who need support and care as they face this challenging illness. Prior to my diagnosis, I had a successful career as a lawyer in private practice. When people think of lawyers, "giver" is probably not the first word that comes to mind. I have done a few charitable deeds along the way, donating legal services, but it probably won't surprise you to hear that my friends haven't encouraged me to redo the monograms on my towels to read "MT2" for the second coming of Mother Teresa. In other words, it's time for me to start giving back.

6. **Tell my story.** Writing this book has been a cathartic experience. I have shared a lot of things beyond the cancer experience itself, though it is not typically in my character to share my true feelings and thoughts. In writing this story, I challenged myself so that I could offer you some hope, a positive outlook, and yes, hopefully, a smile. Maybe this book will inspire you to help a friend or stranger, or they will be inspired to help you. If you have cancer, your cathartic experience might take different forms, such as unloading your fears and challenges with a trained professional, a family member, or a good friend. For me, it was putting pen to paper. At the very least, I hope my story will send you running out the door to get that overdue mammogram. After all, the breast defense is a good offense.

My experience was unique to me. It was the sum of my age, of the totality of my life events prior to cancer, of my environment, and of my family and friends. Yours will be unique to you. I do not expect that your path will mirror mine, nor do I intend to write a prescription for you or to judge your experience. My only hope is that, regardless of how different your story is from mine, this book will uplift your spirits. For many people, their experience has been much worse than mine, and I feel for them each and every step of the way.

One thing we all have in common, though, is that we're in a situation that can cause a lot of stress and heartache. If you are a cancer patient and need to sob uncontrollably from time to time, there are many valid reasons for that, and I would be the last person to judge you for doing so. I would simply hand you a box of Kleenex so you wouldn't have to use your sleeve to wipe your red nose, and listen as you ran your makeup with your tears. But when you're done crying and ready for a smile, dive into this book. I wrote it for you and hope it can offer some comfort as you navigate the road ahead.

Cathy Croshaw

Lake Tahoe, California, August 2019

PART ONE:

The Nudge

CHAPTER 1

LUNCH *and* THEN SOME

"HEY, HOW'VE YOU BEEN? OH my God, your hair looks great. It's gotten so long!" said Jenny as we exchanged hugs and assessed one another's appearance, as only women can do.

"Oh, thanks. I just came from my keratin treatment. You're looking pretty wonderful yourself—did you decide to stop aging?" I quipped.

"Very funny. It's probably just that the kids are out of the house and Mike and I can finally live a peaceful existence, not running ragged every minute of our lives."

We had just met up for lunch, and the hostess was showing us to our table. As soon as we were seated, I launched right into nostalgia.

"I can't believe it's been twenty years," I commented, shaking my head as I looked out the restaurant window at all the kids walking by.

They sauntered out from the high school down the street holding their caramel macchiatos with extra whipped cream. It was midday, and the rest of the pedestrians were primarily well-dressed women with small dogs or women in leggings on the way to yoga.

I thought about how much time had gone by since Jenny and I had first met, and how we ended up at this over-privileged mecca on the peninsula just south of San Francisco. Jenny was also staring out the window, waiting anxiously for our Chardonnay to arrive.

"I know," she said. "So many memories, some good and some bad."

Just a few weeks before my move to Tahoe, I was having lunch at Pizzeria Delfina, the new Italian restaurant in downtown Burlingame, with my dear friend Jenny. The restaurant was packed, and the noise level distracting, but we lucked out and were seated by an open window next to the sidewalk. The noise was less deafening there, and for the most part, we could hear each other. I must have had my hearing aid on that day.

"The kids were so cute when they were little," Jenny reminisced, lost in her memories. Scanning the menu, she caught herself and added, "I mean they're beautiful adults now, of course, but that's a different story. Remember the Fourth of July when Kelly got that new bicycle with pink streamers, and she fell and scraped her knee?"

"I know, that was a huge setback in her enthusiasm for bike riding." I paused as I tried to decide what to order.

"And the neighbors who have come and gone? They say they'll keep in touch, but they never do," Jenny said as she dabbed at her eyes with her napkin.

"Don't mess with me like that, Jenny. We're going to keep in touch, aren't we?" I quickly responded, defensively.

"Yes, we will. Maybe you can stay at our house when you have to come to San Francisco for business."

"I would love that. I can even take care of your screaming cat if you're not home." Jenny's cat made the most horrific noise, which sounded a lot like a baby crying or screeching. Not everyone would volunteer for cat-sitting duty. We cracked ourselves up over the cat.

"I mean, the Chapmans just disappeared off the map. Let's make a pact right now that we will not lose track of each other," I added.

"Okay, as soon as our wine arrives, we'll make a toast to that," Jenny agreed, then continued: "God, I remember how the Chapmans just couldn't understand why their son and all his friends would come into the house and eat everything in sight."

"Yup, until the lightbulb went on, and they realized the boys were getting high in the backyard first," Jenny snickered.

At this point the tears had dried, and we were both laughing outright. After I caught my breath, I added, "And the Gilmores, whose son almost hung up on Harvard admissions because he thought their acceptance call was a prank?"

We both giggled over that. It was clear that we were making a fairly decent contribution to the noise level of the restaurant, as several patrons looked our way.

"And what about the annual river-rafting trip with dozens of Oakland firefighters and most of our local PTA?" Jenny added. "What a combo! Those firefighters sure knew their way around a barbecue. And I gotta say, they were so much more fun than the PTA."

I shook my head. "Were you there for our first trip, when I slept in the beach chair with Kelly after she puked all over the tent we borrowed?"

Jenny cringed at the memory. "Oh yeah. I was surprised that you ever came on that trip again. Good times," she said sarcastically.

Soon after, the waiter arrived to take our order. After he left, I narrowed my eyes.

"Remember that bitch next door who sued Bob and me for parking on the public street in front of her house?" I asked. "That was after we caught her husband teaching their son how to pee on our car. We liked to refer to her as Cruella de Vil when we were being nice. If there is such a thing as bad karma, I really don't want to be her."

Jenny chuckled. "Yes, I have tried to forget about her. Last I heard, she moved to San Francisco, and I hope we never see her again."

"I'll second that. But I think, overall, it was a great neighborhood to raise kids," I said. "I love that everyone knew each other and watched out for each other's kids."

Jenny nodded. "I know. It really *does* take a village."

The sense of community in this neighborhood sometimes made it easy to forget that it was part of a densely populated suburb smack in between San Francisco and Silicon Valley. Just then, our reverie was cut short by the arrival of our salads and, at long last, the Chardonnay.

After the waiter left, Jenny held out her glass, "Cheers! Here's to a lifelong friendship." We clinked glasses, and Jenny headed back down memory lane. "Don't you think, looking back, that it's amazing to see how the kids turned out?"

"It's amazing they all made it through high school," I offered with a sigh of relief.

Jenny nodded, smiling. "Who knew that Ren, the prom queen, would go on to be a biochem major at UCSB? We didn't see that one coming."

"And that your daughter, Meghan, the adorable Pippi Longstocking look-alike, would grow into a beautiful woman rocking the flaming red hair?" I asked.

"Right?" Jenny laughed. "And weren't their high school years the scariest thing you've ever lived through?"

We both grimaced at the thought, me more than Jenny.

"Don't remind me," I said with a pained look on my face. "Remember when the drunk kid tried to crash a party at my house by crawling through the doggie door?" I asked. "He would never have made it past his shoulders, but Kelly thwarted his efforts just as his face peeked through. Then later that night, he ended up naked on your front doorstep? Your kids were so nice to drive him home."

Jenny burst out laughing. Of course, this party had taken place when we were away for the weekend and Kelly was supposedly in the care of another family. But we fell for the classic switcheroo, when one kid says they are staying at a friend's house, and of course, the friend says they are staying at your house, forgetting to mention that you are out of town. By this time the Chardonnay had kicked in. We were enjoying our pasta and had tears streaming down our faces from our raucous laughter. It was only now, a few years after these events, that we could laugh about them.

Pausing a moment to regain my composure, I added, "Oh, and then there was that wonderful teaching moment when Kelly was picked up by the cops, because she was the one carrying the handle of vodka when they arrived. Before that, Bob and I didn't even know what a 'handle' was. Our *children* taught us that it's a bottle of booze so big that it has a built-in handle."

Jenny laughed. "I didn't know what a 'handle' was until just now."

"Yup," I continued. "By the time the kids were in high school, we were learning as much from them as they were from us. We tried to teach them about 'mixers,' the alternative to guzzling straight alcohol. They claimed they couldn't afford mixers. But, of course, they could afford the handle of vodka. We even offered to spring for the orange juice or tonic water ourselves! By that point, we were so worn down by all the teenage shenanigans that once the cops had released Kelly into our custody, we could only manage to say, 'Promise us you won't be the one holding the bottle when the cops arrive next time, okay?' We were certain that the local police force referred to us on a first-name basis by then."

Jenny chuckled and took a deep breath. "Like everyone says, it goes so quickly."

I nodded.

"I can't believe you're leaving," she said. "What's your moving date?"

"In a couple of weeks. It's getting close."

Jenny shifted in her seat and turned serious. "I know this is going to sound weird, but are you current on your mammograms?"

Yes, I thought, *that is a bizarre transition. What would possess her to think of that in the middle of a fun lunch?* I decided to just go with the flow and said: "Nah, I'm a couple years behind, but things have been crazy. I'll do that after we get settled." In fact, I had purposely deferred the mammogram, thinking that I had already been through so many of them and that they were always negative. Why would that change?

"No, do it now," Jenny was insistent.

Between the two of us, Jenny was usually the one who was calm and collected, but I noticed now that her cheeks were flushed, which may or may not have been from the wine. She leaned forward awkwardly over her plate, urging me to get the mammogram done before I left town.

Jesus! I thought. *She is not going to let up.* So I tried to offer her a dose of my reality: "We have fourteen days before we leave. We have to pack, put stuff in storage, clean the house and yard, make arrangements to get the house in Tahoe ready, say goodbye to other neighbors . . . oh, and work and eat and sleep. Where exactly do I fit in the mammogram?"

But Jenny had several friends our age who had gone through breast cancer, so she wasn't going to let me off the hook without a fight.

"You remember Karen?" she pressed. "A year ago she was diagnosed with breast cancer, had to go through chemo and everything. And I hate to mention it, but remember Gail, whose kids were older than yours; she lived over on Castillian? She died from breast cancer when our kids were in elementary school."

I shook my head. How could I forget these neighbors? As I recalled the stories about Jenny's friends, I began to understand why she was not going to let go of this topic. *But did she really have to bring in the heavy artillery right out of the box?*

Jenny met my gaze and did not let go. Her persistence was start-ing to freak me out a little.

Does she know something that I don't? I thought. *Does she get a commission from the Women's Center? Could we just talk about the kids some more?*

Despite my best efforts, I was unable to derail her. She was dead serious as she leaned in closer, in fact, very close to violating my boundaries for personal space. The more she leaned forward, the more I leaned back.

"Please, do this for me," she pleaded. "I don't want to see another friend go through that. I don't want to wonder whether I'll get that phone call after you've moved."

I couldn't help but wonder how that could be worse than receiv-ing the news in person, before I moved, but I didn't dwell on that thought for very long. Given her relentlessness, I was now trying to focus on the gist of the conversation and not sidetrack my thinking with senseless technicalities.

Jenny continued, determined. "Our hospital has the new 3-D imaging equipment. And I'm sure they don't have that where you're going."

I casually took a sip of wine. "I guess that would mean some-thing to me if I knew what a 3-D mammogram was . . ."

Jenny patiently explained that 3-D mammography was the most advanced technology available at the time for the detection of breast cancer. It provided much greater clarity and detail than the 2-D images, which were more difficult to read. She explained that small tumors were often missed by the 2-D technology and that she thought the 3-D method had up to a fifty percent better chance of detecting breast cancer than the 2-D method.

"Oh," I said sheepishly, amazed by my own ignorance. I hadn't realized that my friend was the local authority on all things related to breast cancer. But it made sense given the history of her friends. My resolve was rapidly weakening. I also recalled that Jenny had done the thirty-nine-mile Walk for the Cure a few years back. The topic of breast cancer may have come up a few times during that trek. She was very committed to the cause.

"You know what's really strange?" she asked. "Every June, one of my friends has been diagnosed with breast cancer."

What? I shuddered at this comment. *Did she really just say that?* The *Jaws* soundtrack suddenly started playing in my head. Without hesitation, my mind went to a dark place: *Well, it's June, so obviously it'll either be you or me.*

I knew Jenny had other friends, but it didn't occur to me that she could mean anyone other than the two of us. Don't ask me why. We said our goodbyes and renewed our promise to stay in contact on a regular basis.

I called the Women's Center from the car on the way home from our lunch and tried to schedule my mammogram for sometime before our move. They were booked solid, three weeks out. With my newfound knowledge and sense of urgency, I patiently explained: "I'm moving to a location that doesn't have the 3-D equipment, so I need to do this before I go in two weeks." They understood and agreed to schedule it the day before our move. Had it not been for Jenny, I most likely would have waited another year or so to catch up on my mammograms, which could have led to a very different outcome for this book, and for me.

PART TWO:

The Backstory

CHAPTER 2

I FOUGHT *the* LAW

WHY ARE YOU TORTURING ME with the details of your back-story, you may ask? I'm just reading this book because I want to know about breast cancer. But cancer doesn't occur on paper. It happens to people we know and care about. For that reason, in addition to sharing my cancer experience, I offer you key moments in my life, some of which may help you understand the life that was interrupted by cancer, some of which may have contributed to my cancer, and others that I hope will make you laugh.

I said my story is unique to the sum total of my life experience, and as a result, my life experience comes into play by necessity. My friendship with Jenny and how that developed over the years is central to my diagnosis and treatment path. My relationships in the community where my kids grew up are what made me comfortable with the medical team I was initially assigned. My prior medical history impacted my reaction to having cancer and, in part, contributed to my cancer. You may decide to make different lifestyle choices than I did because of the risks involved. My family and friends were my inner support group, so I want to introduce you to them and the different ways in which they were able to provide that support.

Part of what made cancer treatment bearable to me was being able to use work as a diversion and distraction, but I will only give you the thumbnail version of my career path, because—believe it or not—I understand that not everyone wants to hear the gory details of a lawyer's professional life. Cancer had other ripple effects on my life, and I reluctantly share those with you here. I say reluctantly because some are intensely personal, but if they help one person, they are worth telling. Finally, my impulsive life changes have resulted in my proudest and happiest moments, and I hope that my opportunistic philosophy will also give you food for thought.

* * *

Looking back, sometimes it seems that my entire life was a poorly planned sequence of events, one non sequitur after the next. But poor planning works well for me, and if I had to start over, I wouldn't do things differently.

When I have been asked on occasion to plot out my future in a five-year plan, I've cringed. Fully accepting that I don't fall into the "planner" camp, I prefer to describe myself as opportunistic. Being opportunistic allows me to view a situation and have the flexibility to respond in whatever way I deem appropriate at the time. Consequently, I am not violating any existing plan, which, by definition, is made before you know what the full set of circumstances is going to be.

I know I would not have been a lawyer if I'd had a definite game plan for my life. But by chance, law ended up being my career for thirty-seven long years. Like everything else I have done, it just seemed like the right thing to do at the time.

I grew up in Los Angeles in the 1960s, blissfully unaware that I had acquired a peculiar accent—one later memorialized by Frank Zappa and his daughter Moon Unit in the song "Valley Girl." Having survived all the social trauma that growing up as a Valley Girl entailed, I attended UC Berkeley, where I struggled to ditch the accent. After all, it wasn't going to gain me any respect in an academic community.

I graduated in the late 1970s with a degree in comparative literature and no accent. I decided to major in comparative literature, not to compare literature necessarily but because I liked to read, and I wanted to study more than one language. There was no other major that allowed this opportunity, so I just went with it. I studied French, Spanish, a tiny bit of German, and an even tinier bit of Latin. I also read quite a few things in English.

While I was in college, I had the vague idea that I wanted to do something international, but I had come to the realization that to be a translator or do most careers that required more than one language, I would have to be significantly more fluent in those languages than I was. As much as I wracked my brain, I never pinpointed a specific career that combined my scattered knowledge of all things linguistic. So, shortly before graduation I concluded, much to my horror, that the career path ahead seemed murky unless I wanted to pursue teaching, which required much more patience than I would ever have.

A lot of my friends were finding that their undergraduate liberal arts majors had landed them on an equally ill-defined career path. Political science majors, in particular, were at a similar crossroads when they started thinking about their futures. I noticed that some of my friends were taking the LSAT to see if they could get into law school, so I decided to follow suit.

I woke up on a Saturday morning, with barely a hangover at all, downed a family-sized Snickers bar and a large cup of coffee, and went in to take the test. That was what we did for test prep in those days. No class, no tutor. You just sharpened your pencils, went in, and took your best swing. Since that was the norm, it was a pretty even playing field.

Apparently, my power breakfast did the trick, because I scored high enough to get into a reputable law school. The following year, I attended law school at UC Davis. I was fairly certain that I didn't want to practice law, but I thought a legal education could be helpful for whatever career I'd choose three years later, when I would be older and hopefully wiser.

During the first year of law school, I found myself drowning in the cesspool that is a legal education, having no comprehension of the context of what we were learning and definitely no idea what the answers were—to anything. I dreaded public speaking. And as far as I knew, that was one of the chief qualifications for a good attorney. I had never actually been in a law office by this point, but I'd watched plenty of legal dramas on TV. The problem was, I couldn't see myself competing with Adam and Amanda Bonner (Spencer Tracy and Katherine Hepburn as married lawyers in *Adam's Rib*), Perry Mason, or even Ally McBeal. I guess you could say I was slightly out of my element.

Tragically, because public speaking was my biggest nightmare, I paired up with a guy who shared the same fear for the moot court competition during my first year in law school. This competition replicated an argument before a court of appeal and was either required or possibly the only résumé builder that I could dream up, I don't remember. In any case, because of our trepidation, we over-prepared for the competition to an embarrassing degree, with the disastrous result that we won.

Mortified by our success, we discovered that this esteemed victory meant we would next have to compete publicly, in front of the entire law school, faculty, alumni, and any prospective drop-ins. On the date of the final competition, the auditorium was standing-room only. My partner and I were shaking in our brand-new suits.

As if that weren't enough, the school set up extra monitors in the hallways so that more people could witness our humiliation. My partner had a nervous giggle that he was unable to control if things started going badly. For my part, I would most likely hyperventilate or pass out cold on the floor of the mock courtroom. Fortunately, those things didn't happen. However, our shaky performance made it clear to me that I did not want to do trial work. It may have been less embarrassing in reality than in my imagination, but the stress of participating in the competition took years off my life. Thankfully, we took second place in this public exposition and spared ourselves competition at the statewide level.

Unfortunately, after three years of law school, I still didn't know what I wanted to do career-wise. This is due, in part, to the fact that law school teaches a specific method of learning—how to find information or argue from any perspective whether you believe in it or not—but it's short on teaching substance. I didn't realize at the time that this was purposeful. I had entered law school with some vague notion that I would know "the law" by the time I graduated. But the law isn't a thing, as I found out. It's a moving target, so you can never definitively *learn* it. You can only research it when you need an answer and make your best arguments based on drawing parallels to similar situations. That being the case, when I graduated law school, I did not feel any more qualified for a career than I had when I'd graduated from college. To make matters more interesting, the legal market was in the tank.

Trial and Error

Determined that I should profit from my schooling, or at least obtain some understanding of the real-life application of what I had supposedly learned, I registered to take the bar exam. That way, I could try out being a lawyer for a year or two and see what the field was all about. Turns out, studying for the bar exam is not very exciting. I was, however, introduced to the law school equivalent of Cliff's Notes, and that discovery was groundbreaking. These small books were published by the companies that provide the prep classes for the bar. Our professors had cautioned us during the first week of law school to *never* use these books, but they didn't say why. Now that we were supposed to use them to congeal all the muddy logic that we had soaked up over the past three years, I saw right away why we were not supposed to use them in class: *They had all the answers.* The frustration of realizing that I had scratched my head for weeks over the basic principles of contracts when they were right there on a single page was overwhelming.

One day, a girlfriend and I were determined to get through our preparation for the real-property portion of the exam. Real property suffers from a series of archaic rules, such as the Rule Against Perpetuities and other antiquities. So, we decided to have a sip of Grand Marnier to boost our commitment and inspiration for this portion of our preparation. When we finished the bottle, we had not progressed in our knowledge of real property, but it was much more fun than we had anticipated. The next morning in the bar review class, I asked if she might be interested in a "Breakfast Jack," a greasy specialty of Jack in the Box. She almost hurled on the spot.

I then concluded that I needed a healthier distraction from the tedium of studying for the bar than Grand Marnier. As a better diversion from my studies, I decided to take flying lessons. Davis had a small airport, and the student loan that I had taken out to get to the finish line had not been quite exhausted, so I figured why not?

I soon discovered that flying small planes was a better distraction from studying for the Bar Exam than I had ever dreamed. By the end of the summer, I had my pilot's license and would take a plane out for a couple of hours just to enjoy the freedom of flying. The Davis airport had so little traffic that it was an uncontrolled airport, meaning there was no air traffic control. You basically just get on the radio and say, "I'm landing. Is anyone else out there?" In this environment, flying was a Zen-like meditative experience. As an added bonus, my nominal flying experience led to my first job with a law firm, practicing aviation law. Even though I was a new pilot, there were few female law school graduates with a pilot's license, so I was able to capitalize on the novelty.

My interview for that job consisted of some meetings with several junior members of the law firm and then with Bill, one of the senior partners. Bill was a heavy drinker, a fact that became clear when the interview ended in the bar downstairs from the law office. After my one scotch to Bill's three, I was certain that I had either gotten a job or a date. I was only interested in the job, so at that juncture, I claimed a prior engagement and drove back to UC Davis for a fine Friday-night tradition of watching the TV show *Dallas* with a group of my law school buddies. We didn't really like the show, but it had all the intellectual stimulation we could handle after a week of class, and there were plenty of melodramatic moments in the show that sent us all into gales of laughter.

On the following Monday, the firm where I had just interviewed called, offering me my first job as a lawyer. I immediately went shopping for more suits, professional-looking blouses, and of course, shoes. Even if I didn't really have a clue what lawyers did every day, I was going to show up for my first day on the job looking like one. I may have actually looked more like Elle Woods, Reese Witherspoon's character in *Legally Blonde*, but I couldn't see spending my soon-to-be salary on gray and navy-blue suits. That's just not my style.

Of course, my dream job would have been in real estate or corporate law, where I wouldn't be onstage embarrassing myself as I had imagined I had done during the aforementioned moot court debacle. But in the tight job market, those were the jobs claimed by people who graduated way higher in their class than I had. So, I ended up practicing aviation law, where I initially worked on high-stakes lost-baggage claims.

During this time, I learned that nearly half the claimants asserted they had lost their grandmother's priceless jewelry, which always had incalculable sentimental value, in their Samsonite luggage. The similarity of the stories might have been the reason that the airlines didn't just pay off the claims in the first place and, instead, chose to challenge them, turning me—their legal bulldog—loose on the unsuspecting consumers. Okay, to be honest, I looked about twelve years old and had to be very creative to intimidate anyone at this stage. I was the female legal equivalent of Doogie Howser.

After a few of these claims, I became a little bit cynical. On one occasion, I took a call from the attorney on the other side and started off with "Let me guess: Your client's grandmother's priceless jewelry was in the bag?"

"How did you know that?" came the response from the opposing attorney.

"Cuz everyone loses grandma's priceless jewelry," I responded sarcastically. I was able to settle that case for peanuts once the attorney realized how transparent the claim was.

Eventually, I graduated to work on cases involving small plane crashes, helicopter crashes, and even one commercial airline crash. These were far more interesting, as they involved real damage and real injuries. The challenge was to determine the cause and liability for what had occurred. My most memorable plane crash case involved a new pilot with about two hundred hours of flying experience. I could relate to this minimal level of qualification as a pilot, since that was about the number of hours I had. Sadly, he took off in the fog with no experience in using the instruments required when you can't see where you're going. He crashed into a mountain. My firm represented the aviation insurance company that was sued by his heirs.

The first thing we noticed was that the pilot's insurance application stated he had ten thousand hours of flying experience, roughly fifty times the experience he appeared to have. A bold misrepresentation of this magnitude would automatically void the insurance policy. The lawyer on the other side, however, developed a creative theory positing that the pilot actually *did* have ten thousand hours of flying experience but that after the crash, a bear had eaten the pilot's logbook containing the record of all his hours. The "dog ate my homework" defense didn't impress either the judge or the jury. Suffice it to say, we won that trial.

In an aviation practice, I was often up against lawyers who were seasoned military pilots with thousands of hours of flying experience. They would frequently challenge my qualifications and imply that I knew nothing about airplanes. Not one to be intimidated, all I had to say was that I, too, was a pilot, and they backed down, never challenging me further to find out that I only had a couple of hundred hours of experience and really didn't know anything about airplanes.

After a few years of aviation work, though, I quit flying, coming to the wise conclusion that unless you have a reason to fly frequently enough that your reactions become intuitive, you probably just shouldn't fly at all. It was a recurring theme in many of the crashes that I litigated, and I decided to apply it to my own life as well.

When I was no longer flying, the aviation work pretty much lost its charm, but I still wasn't sure what I wanted to do when I grew up. I enjoyed the diversity of a law practice in which no two days were ever the same. I had survived the first couple of years, where I'd been completely lost, and finally felt as if I had a few marketable skills. I loved writing, analyzing, researching, problem-solving, and socializing with colleagues, clients, and even opponents.

At this juncture, I took a job with another law firm. I am now embarrassed to say that I defended insurance companies for an entire decade. Initially, it was the really awful stuff, with large companies throwing their weight around against individuals. Later on, though, I represented insurance companies in battles against Fortune 500 companies. At least that was more of a fair fight.

CHAPTER 3

EMERGING FROM *the* FOG

The Townhouse

I bought my first home while out on a shoe-shopping excursion. It was bound to happen, given my propensity for impulse buys and general lack of planning. Throughout the 1980s, I regularly traveled up to Marin County from San Francisco, either on bike rides or to shop. But the shopping and bike rides were just a means to an end. My true goal was more purposeful: to escape the fog. During this time, I lived in San Francisco's Marina District, in the shadow of the Golden Gate Bridge. All summer long, the fog rolled under the bridge to darken my neighborhood. I was finding it unbearable, as the freezing temperatures and swirling wind often left me in a deep funk. This was around the time I was beginning to understand that daylight was an essential part of my emotional well-being.

Leaving the mall one day on one of my fog runaways, I toured some townhomes in a new development. From my bike rides and shopping trips, I knew that this location was right where the fog stopped and the sun came out. I like to think that I stopped at the development completely on a lark, but it was reminiscent of my childhood, where every Sunday we would tour open houses. Often, we would buy one, resulting in our family moving quite frequently. However, I was "not in the market and had no money for a down payment," as I told the nice sales lady, but I really liked the townhomes.

She knew an impulse buyer when she saw one and said, "Let's talk."

She proposed a deal where I could put almost nothing down and purchase the townhome. Half an hour later, I made an offer. I ran out of the sales office as fast as I could, hoping they would not realize that I was financially unfit to buy the home. I called my most scattered friend, Jennifer, to share the news, certain that she, if anyone, would be excited.

Instead, she screamed, "Are you nuts? You didn't even look at anything else? What were you thinking?" After she berated me for ten minutes, we agreed that she and I would visit open houses in the area the next day to figure out how big a mistake I was making. We toured everything within a ten-mile radius that was close to the same price range. At the end of the day, Jennifer sheepishly muttered, "You bought the right thing." Her approval was nice, but all I really cared about was the opportunity to leave the fog behind.

When the bank approved my loan, I was incredulous, given my historic inability to save a dime. Elated that I would be allowed to purchase something as substantial as a new townhome, I hurried to sign the papers before the bank could figure out who they were dealing with.

Bob

At this phase in my life, I met Bob. The law firm where I was working at the time had imploded. Picture a divorce with sixty parties instead of two, and all sixty are lawyers. It was not an amicable split. At the lowest point in this fiasco, three men cried in my office in the span of one week, all on separate occasions. I offer this detail only as an illustration of how emotionally devastating this kind of split can be. Trust was breached, lies were told, and a lot of people and careers were caught in the crossfire.

In the aftermath of the split, which occurred late in the year, I called home to tell my mom that I would not be home for Christmas. I was emotionally drained and just needed some time to myself. A large group of attorneys, including me, was planning to leave the existing firm at the beginning of the year, and I needed to marshal my energy to endure the rest of the ordeal. My mom wasn't happy about my missing Christmas but said she understood. She hurried to get off the phone before I could tell whether or not she was crying.

To decompress, I went skiing at Squaw Valley in Lake Tahoe and stayed at a shared house that I had joined for the ski season. Joining the house was an inexpensive way to be able to ski as much as possible, without paying for a hotel, and to meet a few people along the way. My shared house was a stone's throw from the Squaw Valley ski resort and was not overly fancy, just spacious and comfortable, which was exactly what I was looking for. Ever since I had learned to ski in college, I'd loved the sport for the speed, social life, and natural beauty of the mountain surroundings. Having been raised in Los Angeles, snow was a novelty, and I couldn't get enough of it. I could ski with groups of friends or solo, and I didn't hesitate to drive up to Tahoe on my own for a little downtime whenever the mood struck me.

That Christmas of 1989 was my first trip to the mountains to enjoy the benefits of the shared house. Around this time, I had concluded that my personal relationships were just as disastrous as my work ones, so I'd sworn off dating. Nothing operates as more of a dating magnet than this type of resignation and disinterest. When you genuinely, completely don't care and are not looking, men crawl out of the woodwork. It's almost as good as cruising the block with a new puppy.

This began to dawn on me on my first day skiing when I stopped in at the Waffle House for breakfast. As fate would have it, two good-looking ski instructors were seated at the table next to me. I noticed a neatly folded newspaper on the edge of their table and asked if I could borrow it with no thought in my mind other than I wanted to read the newspaper, and they appeared to be finished with theirs. One of the guys, Brian, smiled and handed me the paper. Soon after, we started talking, and Brian asked if I would like to ski with him for the day.

I figured no harm could come of it, so I agreed. At the very least, I would have a free ski lesson. At first, I was slightly intimidated at the thought of skiing with an instructor. To be honest, though, Brian was a good, but not great, skier, so the intimidation soon wore off. Throughout the day, I learned that Brian was a stockbroker from the Bay Area who also taught skiing on the weekends. He was twenty-eight, and I was in my early thirties at the time. As soon as I turned thirty, I had decided that I was old enough to date a younger man, since by then a younger man could be gainfully employed. In my early twenties, that was not likely to be the case, so I didn't venture into younger territory.

Brian and I skied together the entire day. We laughed about the friend he had ditched at the Waffle House and shared a beer at the end of the day. Since we had such a blast skiing, we planned to go to dinner together later that evening. When I went back to the shared house to change, I noticed there was another guy there. It was Bob, but he was arm in arm with two women he had just met at the bar.

Apparently, he had bet them that he was older than they were and won the bet. The "losers," as I politely referred to the girls, had to buy him dinner. Dick, another participant in the shared house, thought Bob should share his bounty, so when Dick's girlfriend passed out on the sofa from one too many hotbuttered rums, he joined Bob and the two ladies for dinner. I made a cautious assessment that Bob seemed like a nice guy, but Dick? Dick was total slime, both for bringing the girlfriend who passed out on the couch and then for abandoning her for two other girls.

During the brief interlude back at the house, I began to wonder if I was, once again, starting down the path of a worthless relationship with Brian. I was determined not to go there. If I was going to be in any relationship at this point, it would have to be on my terms: no game playing, no lying. We'd just like each other or we wouldn't. I was simply too exhausted to cater to anyone else or to deal with any shenanigans. Reminding myself of my resolve, I changed into my jeans, a casual but bright aqua top (to match my equally bright aqua ski parka), and after-ski boots. The top and parka were luminescent enough to draw attention away from the Christmas tree. I've always believed that there's no rule that casual also has to be understated.

When Brian arrived to take me to dinner, Bob and I found ourselves alone in the kitchen for a moment. I casually glanced in Bob's direction and took note of this handsome and confident young man. *What was his story?* I wondered. Before I could get lost in my thoughts, Bob introduced himself, then pointed to Brian out in the living room: "Who are you trying to kid?" he said jokingly, noting that the ski instructor was several years younger than I was.

Dodging a direct answer to his bold question, I responded with an equally bold question: "Where'd you get the two bimbos?" We both grinned, appreciating the momentary banter, and left the kitchen to attend to our respective dates.

My dinner date didn't end well. Dinner itself was fine, but while we were waiting for the bill, Brian excused himself, ostensibly to go to the men's room. Ten or maybe fifteen minutes went by, and I started to grow impatient. My sharply honed instincts raised a red flag as I realized that, unless he had just come down with the stomach flu, he'd been gone way too long. In that moment, I decided that since we had driven to the restaurant in my car and I had the keys, I was done with Mr. Brian the ski instructor, and I stood up to leave.

As I headed for the door, I ran into Brian on the pay phone by the exit (yes, this was before cell phones). He was talking very softly to someone, making lots of excuses and apologizing to whoever was on the other end of the phone. When he saw me, he hung up quickly and started to apologize to me. Brian suddenly struck me as someone who got through life by apologizing rather than doing the right thing in the first place.

"Oh, I should have told you. There's this girl, and we were involved . . ."

Not in the mood for games, I cut him off. I was not in the market for any more emotional trauma and just wanted to cut my losses and go back to the house.

"Look," I said, "I don't give a crap why you're doing this, but you were rude to me and left me sitting at dinner while you were talking with some other woman on the phone."

Brian stared back at me, speechless, perhaps unused to someone shutting him down mid-apology.

"We're done," I added, matter-of-factly. "But if you're super nice to me, I'll drive you back to your car."

Brian nodded and picked up the bill, careful not to say anything that might set me off. The ride back to his car was long and silent.

Since Brian held up his end of the deal, I dropped him off at his car and then drove back to the shared house. When I got back, Bob was sitting on the sofa, talking with Dick and the charming hot-buttered-rum lady, who had woken up long enough to pour herself another drink. The bimbos had left the scene.

From the look on his face, I could tell that Bob was hoping to be rescued from this couple, so I joined them. After the couple started making out on the sofa in front of us, I saw why he needed to be rescued. During our conversation, Bob asked if I would like to ski with him the next day. I didn't want to seem overeager, so I said that Brian had lessons to teach all day, so that shouldn't be a problem. I didn't see any point in providing the details of my failed dinner date or even mentioning that Brian was no longer in the picture.

Bob and I had a great time, which was no surprise after our spirited exchange in the kitchen the night prior. As we talked, we realized that my roommate in the shared house had gone on a couple of dates with Bob previously. That was awkward but also struck us as very funny. Things went so well that we skied together for the next two days. It turned out that Bob was also coming out of a traumatic situation and was in a "no BS" kind of mood, just as I was. On the evening of our last day skiing, Bob's brother and sister-in-law stopped in Tahoe on their way to the Bay Area. We all went to dinner, had a couple of glasses of wine, and laughed about his brother's transition from a strict Mormon upbringing to owning a vineyard.

Bob's brother was also a lawyer, so we, of course, exchanged a few lawyer jokes. I offered my favorite, which was a sad reflection of the times: "There are three women lawyers being considered for partnership and only one partnership spot available. The existing partners decide to slip an extra thousand dollars into each of their paychecks, just to see what they will do. One decides not to mention it and hopes no one will notice. Another runs around the office polling the other young attorneys as to what she should do. The third tells the partners of the mistake in her paycheck. Soooo . . . ," I said in a dramatic buildup: "Which one gets the partnership? [heavy pause, drum roll] The one with the biggest boobs!" Gales of laughter ensued.

The next day, we all went cross-country skiing together. Of the four of us, I was the only novice at this sport, so I spent a lot of time in the snow, watching the others gracefully ski past me. I was okay on the skis as long as the ground was completely level and I didn't have to turn. But sadly, there were ups and downs and curves, so the snow and I became very familiar with each other. Fortunately, we stopped along the way at a cozy little hut for cookies and hot chocolate so I could take a rest and dry off a little before we resumed skiing. Just as I was beginning to get the hang of it, we returned to our starting point, turned in our ski equipment, and called it a day.

The first few days that Bob and I had spent together had been unusually relaxed yet exciting. We'd covered a lot of ground in a short amount of time: I'd already met the family and learned a new sport, and our first date wasn't even over yet. Before our return home, Bob asked me if I had any plans for New Year's Eve. Having only dated jerks in the past, I had expected the game playing to kick in around this time. This was when the guy would either disappear with a dismissive "I'll call you" or explain how much fun the last few days had been but that he needed to get back to work or his girlfriend or wife and kids, whatever. But, what do you know, before ending the first date, Bob had upped the ante and asked for the second date on New Year's Eve, the biggest date night of the year. This telegraphed clearly that he was not married and probably did not even have another girlfriend.

So, I replied nonchalantly: "Not yet."

"How would you like to come with me up to my brother's house in Napa?" he asked.

I pretended to mull this over for a few seconds, then replied: "Great, count me in."

On New Year's Eve day, Bob picked me up at my townhome, and we drove up to Napa together. The four of us cooked a gourmet dinner of beef bourguignon, artichokes with garlic aioli, and truffle risotto, with a Grand Marnier soufflé for dessert. We consumed multiple bottles of wine and champagne, and by the time we got to the soufflé, it was three in the morning.

By then, our sense of formality was nonexistent, as was our ability to transfer the soufflé to dessert plates, so we grabbed four large spoons and ate the dessert straight out of the dish. On New Year's Day, still recovering from the night before, we moved the party to a bar on Main Street in Calistoga and watched the Rose Bowl. Yet another magical date. Looking back, 1989 was my year for swift, life-changing decisions. I guess it's befitting that, on a whim, I decided to take a chance on Bob and spend New Year's Eve with him the same year that I'd bought the townhouse on impulse. Bob was somewhat appalled to hear the shoe-shopping townhome-buying story on the way back from Napa, but fortunately he weighed the odds and, a year later, decided to marry me anyway.

CHAPTER 4

JENNY *and* MIKE:
The EARLY DAYS

ABOUT A YEAR AFTER BOB and I were married, we attended a law conference in Palm Beach, Florida. I had always wanted to be a spouse at a convention, but instead Bob got to enjoy that role. On the first day of the conference, he was invited to a flower-arranging class with the other spouses. Let's just say that even in the early 1990s, the conference was organized by an older and unenlightened group that still believed all the lawyers would be men. In fact, at the conference, I struck up a conversation with a gentleman in his eighties.

He looked at me and said, "Yes, we've had quite a few women members, but none of them stayed." If he had actually been interested in why they hadn't stayed, I probably could have helped him out. Unfortunately, the collective attitude of the men in the group was straight out of the Stone Age.

On the first day, I played golf with a group of three guys in a tournament organized for the conference. One of the attendees scowled and went into a bit of a funk when he saw that there was a woman in the foursome. On the first hole, I outdrove him by about fifty yards. He broke into a huge smile, walked over, and apologized.

"I'm so sorry for being a jerk, but I thought this would be like playing with my wife," he said. Even though I felt bad for his wife, we ended up laughing over his snarky attitude, and after the conference, he actually became a client.

Bob and I met Mike and Jenny at this conference. Mike and I had worked only a couple of blocks from one another in San Francisco in the same field of law, but ironically, we hadn't met until he and I presented a session at the same conference. Turns out, we hit it off, and—after we co-presented our dreadfully boring panel about the finer points of insurance coverage—Mike and I joined Bob and Jenny for dinner. With our business obligations met and our speaking engagements out of the way, Mike and I were ready to stir up some fun. Bob had been bored all day since he didn't yet know anyone from this group and most of the other spouses were busy at the flower-arranging lesson that he'd skipped.

During dinner, we talked about going on some sort of excursion the next day. For some reason, the guys thought deep-sea fishing was the thing to do. I had lost all interest in fishing as a child when my brother accidentally cast his line in my direction and landed a barbed hook in the middle of my back. I also felt bad for the fish when the hooks were removed from their mouths, and of course, cleaning fish was a nonstarter. As far as I could tell, Jenny had a similar distaste for the sport. So Jenny and I had no intention of fishing, but we wanted to spend the day on the ocean and were willing to try something new. We knew that the four of us would have a good time together, so in our complete ignorance of what deep-sea fishing entailed, we agreed to take a "three-hour cruise." In hindsight and being a fan of *Gilligan's Island*, I should have known that this three-hour cruise was doomed from the start.

Bob and I met Jenny and Mike for breakfast the next morning. Jenny and I were dressed in stylish white shorts and blouses and both had on floppy sun hats. We had brought books to read if we ran out of things to talk about. Exchanging compliments on our outfits, we were ready for a day in the sun, lounging on the deck, while the boys did their thing.

After breakfast, the four of us enthusiastically boarded the boat. It was just us and our captain-and-fishing-guide. Jenny and I were really looking forward to the outing, but our hopes were soon dashed. The first thing we noticed was that the floppy hats just had to go. As soon as the boat accelerated, we lunged to catch them before they flew off. We also noticed that the boat did not appear to have a deck made for lounging in the sun. Soon after, we were shocked to discover that it also did not have a bathroom. Had we known that, we probably would have severely cut our coffee consumption at breakfast. This trip was starting to look a lot different from what we had imagined.

The farther out we went, the stronger the wind became. Why hadn't the guys mentioned this when we showed up for breakfast in completely inappropriate attire? Surely, they would have known. Before long we realized that our stylish shorts would be permanently stained when the slimy, greasy fish stains we found all over the boat transferred to our once-pristine white shorts. Our dressy blouses suddenly felt silly and out of place as well. We accepted the fact that we would not look glorious on the boat but would instead be battling the wind and sea for the next few hours. Resigned to our fates, we put on jackets to prepare for the ordeal and took up our posts leaning against the cabin in the cockpit of the boat, where we stayed for the duration of the trip.

Jenny and I spent the first half hour out of the harbor laughing over our misconception of deep-sea fishing. I learned that Mike was an avid fly fisherman and that Jenny had spent many long days waiting patiently on shore as Mike fished. Jenny also talked about her three kids. All three were under the age of six at the time, so the opportunity to have some time with Mike at the conference, without the kids in tow, was a rare treat. We talked about our homes in the Bay Area. At the time, we lived in Greenbrae in Marin County, just a few miles north of San Francisco. Jenny and her family lived a few miles south of the San Francisco Airport in San Mateo. I'd heard of San Mateo but had not spent any time there.

Maybe half an hour into the trip, we were in rough seas, and Jenny and I had both turned green. At that point, our conversation came to a screeching halt. When the captain offered us tuna fish sandwiches, we almost lost it, since we were both already struggling not to feed the fish, and the prospect of actually *eating* fish was almost enough to push us over the edge. Suffice it to say, when we finally got back to shore, Jenny and I raced to be the first off the boat.

So much for new adventures.

Mike and Bob

The men had fared better, however. Bob had caught a three-foot sea bass, and Mike proudly held up a tiny sardine as his catch of the day. Sadly, we had no way to cook the bass at the hotel, so we ended up giving both away to the local fishermen. They were thrilled to have the fish and laughed hysterically in the background while I took a photo of Bob and Mike with their catch.

We had dinner at the resort that night with Mike and Jenny and two other couples. Dinner dredged up many fish tales, with Bob and Mike spreading their arms wide to show the other guys at the table the size of the fish they'd caught. Jenny and I had recovered by then and shared our side of the fishing trip with the other women at the table.

I remember saying, "Yeah, Jenny and I were chatting away on the boat, and suddenly Jenny got really quiet. She looked at me and whispered, 'If I hurl off the boat, which side should I choose?'"

At which everyone laughed.

Jenny smiled sheepishly as I continued. "Downwind, of course," I said, pointing to the right to show everyone the appropriate side of the boat.

I could tell the others at the table were entertained, so I leaned in closer and added, "Then, I realized she was in pretty bad shape. I turned to her and said, 'You're not okay, are you?' Jenny just shook her head. Meanwhile, I was feeling marginally better than Jenny, dishing out sympathy and advice to try to help her out. In an act of sheer selflessness, I offered hair-holding services, if needed. After trying to get her to focus on the horizon, I noticed that her color was already changing. I tried a pressure point on her wrist to see if she could get some relief, and that's when I started to feel queasy myself. From then on, we were both struggling."

Everyone giggled as I shared our ordeal. The other women expressed relief that they had chosen the Palm Beach shopping tour as their activity for the day.

"Oh my God," remarked Beth, one of the other wives. "I can't believe you guys actually agreed to join them for that outing. Deep-sea fishing *always* means rough seas and a miserable ride."

"Where were you last night when we needed you?" I asked, and everyone laughed.

Jenny picked up the story where I had left off.

"So Cathy and I demand almost simultaneously: 'Turn this freakin' boat around! We've had enough!' When Bob and Mike looked back at us, they politely asked the captain to head back to port before things got ugly. Fortunately, he obliged, and we made it back to shore in time."

I took over. "As soon as we could disembark, I shouted 'terra firma!' and gleefully hopped off the boat. Jenny kissed the ground when it was her turn! Then we headed for the nearest bar for a medicinal beer. We spent the rest of the afternoon giggling at the bar, celebrating our survival. We were so proud that neither one of us had actually tossed our cookies."

When we finished dinner and headed back to our rooms, I turned to Jenny.

"Oh my God, what a day. Tomorrow, let's just play backgammon or something."

Jenny nodded, and the guys laughed as we said our good-nights.

The next day, Mike and Bob played golf. Jenny and I were determined to get our lounging and reading in and so spent the day by the pool with our books. For the rest of the trip, we didn't feel particularly adventurous and just stayed close to the hotel. The four of us really bonded over this trip, and by the time we were saying our goodbyes, it was clear that Jenny, Mike, Bob, and I would still be friends long after the conference.

CHAPTER 5

MOVIN' *to the* 'BURBS

TWO YEARS LATER, WE ALL went to another conference, this time in Sun Valley, Idaho. By then, our first daughter, Ren, had been born, and she came along as well. The relationship between our two families was pretty much cemented when all of our kids got the flu from the conference day-care facility and Ren barfed nonstop for the better part of the conference. The other kids barfed off and on, but they simply could not live up to the standard that Ren had set.

When I picked Ren up from day care on the first day of the conference, the worker told me, "She had diarrhea all day, so we gave her french fries." Not interested in debating her novel yet idiotic attempt to find a cure for Ren's malaise, Jenny and I headed to the nearest drug store to find a more appropriate solution. After giving Ren and Jenny's kids some Gatorade, Pepto Bismol, and bland food, we put them to bed. Day care was no longer a desirable option for Ren, so Bob took over the day care for the rest of that conference.

A couple of days later, the road trip back home was pretty memorable too, with stops approximately every half hour for Ren to hurl by the side of the road. The day after we got home was

Ren's first birthday. We had planned to throw her a party but had to postpone it when Bob and I came down with the flu ourselves. Instead of celebrating, we put Ren in the crib next to our bed and didn't move all day.

When we had recovered, I touched base with Jenny. Her kids were still sick, and Mike and Jenny had gotten the flu too. *Yet another bonding experience*, I thought with some trepidation as I began to wonder whether every memorable experience with Jenny would involve nausea or worse, actual puking. I sincerely hoped that it wouldn't. Two weeks later, we hosted a birthday party in the park for Ren and took lots of pictures, hoping to create the appearance of a delightful first birthday—despite the fact that she had spent the actual day sick as a dog, imprisoned in her crib.

The following year the four of us were desperate to create better memories than the ones indelibly etched in our brains from the infamous Sun Valley conference, so we planned dinner at Jenny's house. By that time, our second daughter, Kelly, had been born, and we had begun to consider moving from our hillside home in Marin County.

Kelly was an adventurer and a climber. It was not far-fetched to imagine her climbing the railing on the back deck of our home and tumbling down the thirty-foot drop to the hill below. My mom, master of the guilt trip, informed me when our children were born that "there's no such thing as an accident." I correctly understood that to mean that any childhood injury is the fault of the parents. So, with our guilty mindset in place, Bob and I started hunting for the perfect *Leave It to Beaver* neighborhood with flat, tree-lined streets and possibly even a white picket fence. We wanted a place better-suited for raising children—like the neighborhood Jenny and Mike lived in. Driving up to their house for dinner that evening and passing several kids on bicycles and others playing basketball in their driveways, we started exchanging knowing looks. The streets were flat, and they were indeed lined with oak trees. The homes were built in the 1930s and had a lot of character. The yards were, at a minimum, nicely manicured, and some, like Mike and Jenny's, were outright beautiful. Gardening was one of Mike's passions.

Many of the homes in the neighborhood had been remodeled at least once. One feature that we didn't appreciate until later was that most of the remodels involved removing at least one space in the tandem garages. More often than not, the remaining space was used for storage. The unanticipated benefit from this was that virtually everyone parked in the street. You could see people coming and going, and more importantly, people were outside and could regularly connect with each other. Admittedly, sometimes this was a curse, because it was hard to sneak into the house without engaging in a conversation, but it contributed to the feel of a closely connected community. As an added bonus, the elementary school, middle school, and high schools were all within three blocks of the neighborhood, and all had fantastic reputations. By the time we arrived at Mike and Jenny's house, we acknowledged to each other that this could be the neighborhood.

The Bay Area real estate market at the time was robust, to say the least. Many houses were sold by word of mouth before they were even listed on the market. The sellers were holding all the cards, and the listing prices were just a starting point. Any serious offer had to be way above that, kind of like a silent auction. Having someone in the area to keep an ear to the ground was essential. Not ones to waste time, after dinner we declared our intentions to relocate close to Mike and Jenny's home.

"Is this neighborhood as good as it looks? We think this is *exactly* what we're looking for. We'd love it if you would let us know if you hear about anything coming on the market," we were sure to add. Jenny and Mike both assured us that this neighborhood was, in fact, a great place to raise kids.

They were excited at the prospect of having us as neighbors. Jenny filled us in on how great the schools were, except possibly the middle school, which was always dicey, considering the traumas and changes children that age experience. They let us know which kindergarten teacher to request and that the elementary school was maxing out on enrollment. To secure a spot in kindergarten, parents lined up on the sidewalk at 4:00 a.m. or earlier on a designated day and waited anxiously to see if their kid would make it in.

As luck would have it, within a week Jenny called to say that a couple down the street was planning to list their home for sale. Before we had even seen the home, Jenny and Mike planned a welcoming party for us. It was a little premature, but we were still flattered and excited. It was such a different experience from the neighborhood we were leaving. We called the realtor right away to ask if we could see the house before it went on the market. We toured the home the next day and fell in love with it. We just had that feeling that it was *the one*. The realtor insisted on putting the home on the market, presumably so that we would know there would be competing offers. The next day was going to be the open house where the local real estate brokers had a chance to preview the house. After that, multiple offers were expected. We got the message and made an offer on the spot, well above asking price.

Apparently, it was enough to appease the realtor, who said she would be in touch after the seller had an opportunity to review our offer. It took about twenty-four hours for the seller to accept, just hours after the open house. In the meantime, we sweated bullets and talked about our moving date as well as how fun it would be to teach the kids to ride bikes here and what the commute and schools would be like. With Mike and Jenny just a few houses away, we knew we would already have friends in the neighborhood, and there was that welcoming party to look forward to . . . So, when we learned that the sellers had accepted our offer, we pretty much felt as if we'd just won the lottery.

Our elation was short-lived, soon to be replaced by the overwhelming logistics of packing and moving, all while keeping tabs on a one-year-old and three-year-old and holding full-time jobs. We had a thirty-day escrow, so we had to scramble to get packed in time. On the night before the move, we were finally ready, just waiting for the moving van to arrive the next day. As we were collapsing into bed, a mouse skittered across the floor of our bedroom. The chances of me sleeping in a room with a loose mouse were zero, so Bob bravely chased the mouse while I hid in the bathroom.

After a few minutes, he triumphantly announced, "Got him!" Then he walked outside with the shoebox he'd used to capture the mouse. He came back in and dusted off his hands with a proud look of accomplishment on his face. I tentatively left the safety of the bathroom, beaming with pride at my knight in shining armor. Ten minutes later, however, another mouse scurried across the bedroom floor. Clearly, all the moving activity had stirred up an entire family of mice, which must have been living in the walls.

"Bob!" I screamed. "We need to take the kids and stay in a hotel. We can't sleep here. God knows how many little rodents have taken up residence!"

Bob sat calmly on the edge of the bed and shot me his most sincere look.

"I have a confession to make."

"Huh?" I wondered.

"There was no mouse in the shoebox."

I sighed. *Now we're back down to one mouse—not a herd—minus a knight in shining armor.* I stood on the bed while Bob renewed his pursuit of the mouse in earnest, feeling a lot like Lucy and Desi. I screamed every once in a while, just because. Finally, the mouse showed his pointy little face, and Bob beat the life out of him with an umbrella.

This only incited more screaming and crying.

"You weren't supposed to hurt him!" I wailed.

Bob looked at me sheepishly, feeling bad to have finished off the innocent rodent and frustrated that his attempts to humanely remove him from the premises unharmed had failed. Once I had recovered from seeing the small, lifeless body on my bedroom floor, and to make up for all my theatrics, I heaped praise on Bob for his courageous efforts. After all, I had put him in a no-win situation: When the mouse had been loose, I'd insisted we had to look for a hotel, and once it had been pummeled to death—certainly eliminating the chance that it would run across the floor again—I'd been horrified. I slept with one eye open that night, listening for the pitter-patter of tiny little feet.

CHAPTER 6

The LAST STRAW

AROUND THE TIME WE WERE considering a move to the 'burbs, I was working as a trial attorney, handling environmental insurance coverage cases. These were typically cases pitting large manufacturers, oil companies, and other polluters against their insurers. In the smallest of these cases, millions of dollars were at stake. In the largest, billions would be on the line. Regardless of case size, the issue in question was always whether the polluter paid for the cleanup of some environmental disaster or the insurers footed the bill. This was surprisingly interesting, because the law was very new in this area, and each trial would determine the fate of hundreds of similar cases.

But when my daughters were born, I could no longer justify the time, stress, and singled-minded focus that trial requires. Ask any spouse of a trial attorney, and they will unanimously tell you that it is no fun to be around an attorney when they are preparing for or are in the midst of a trial. They can become antisocial, self-absorbed, crabby, and short-tempered. They have no time or patience for anyone else, because they are so busy trying to cram as much information as they can into their brains. They will rattle off the minutia of facts of the case and assume that everyone is just as fascinated by their phenomenal insights as they are. Just before the trial begins, the lawyer is gripped by flaming insecurity and the inexplicable need to rehearse all their most jaw-dropping arguments in front of their defenseless spouse as a testing ground. Trial preparation will fill whatever amount of time you allow it to, and most attorneys will spend every waking hour to prepare. Yet, no matter how much time is invested, there is always that sinking feeling the attorney on the other side knows more than you do, resulting in the paranoid certainty that there is a hidden potential for surprise under every rock. Surprises, as you can imagine, are not good in a trial. During the trial itself, it's better for everyone's sake if these attorneys have no human contact whatsoever outside of the courtroom.

My last trial, which took place in Portland, Oregon, when my daughters were just one and three, lasted five grueling months. Looking back, it was the proverbial straw that broke this camel's back. When I learned that the entire trial had been rendered moot by a ruling that the judge made at the end of trial, I almost lost it. All the personal sacrifices I had made to participate in this fiasco were, in the end, worthless. I had worked every day from 5:00 a.m. to midnight. Then I would return home on Friday night, only to leave again on Sunday to prepare for the following week, all while living a bizarre existence in what is known as "corporate housing."

Corporate housing consists of apartments intended for short-term rentals by executives or professionals who are away from home for extended periods of time, as I was. However, I quickly learned that most of the residents were men freshly kicked out of their homes, awaiting their divorces and relocation to permanent housing. That, in itself, created a rather strange environment for me. If one of them tried to strike up a conversation, I just glared them down. After all, I was married, which they could tell from my wedding ring, and I had no time to waste on small talk.

The décor in my unit was vintage early 1970s with puke-green shag carpet and white walls. A green-and-mustard floral polyester bedspread completed the unsettling picture. The kitchen was tiny, which was fine, since I had no time to cook. For the duration of the trial, the closest I came to a home-cooked meal was a microwaved Lean Cuisine. I had no time to go grocery shopping. My paralegal was able to do that for me, and I just ate whatever she bought. Every waking moment was spent either in court, meeting with attorneys and witnesses, or preparing questioning for the next day.

Throughout the trial, I worked closely with an eccentric scientist who was one of the sloppiest people I have ever had the pleasure to spend time with. He was also a chatterbox and loved to expound on his scientific theories about the case, especially after a couple of vodka tonics. By the time the case started, I was familiar enough with his theories that I did not need to hear them every day. My only desire was that he act like a child in the 1950s and be seen and not heard. I also worked with a local attorney who was my stabilizing force and became a good friend. For a California attorney to try a case in Oregon, you need a local attorney. They act more or less in the role of a sponsor. In my case, he shared the workload and was a tremendous sounding board throughout the trial. In addition to schmoozing with the judge and other attorneys, all of whom knew each other well, his job was to talk me down from the ceiling when we had a bad day in court or when the scientist had one too many and wouldn't stop talking.

One morning, when I found a long-abandoned slice of pizza in a box of documents in my apartment (left there, no doubt, by the eccentric scientist) and discovered that the same scientist had run off to go sailing, locking the exhibits that I needed for the week in his apartment, I made a frank observation that my life sucked.

In retrospect, this was already clear, based on the fact that I was spending an inordinate amount of time away from my family and home, working my butt off so I could be onstage eight hours a day. I had no time whatsoever to myself, not even to take my clothes to the dry cleaner, which was downstairs in my apartment building. In the end, the trial didn't count. The judge's ruling after trial struck me as the ultimate cop-out, as it could easily have been made before the trial had started and spared us all the time, expense, and stress of conducting such a lengthy and complex proceeding. I suspected that the judge was hoping the trial would unfold in such a way where he wouldn't ever have to make a decision, which would definitely lead to an appeal and put his reasoning in the limelight. No good can come from the second-guessing a court of appeal might apply to a decision which seemed appropriate to the trial judge.

At the end of the day, the case settled before it got to the court of appeal, and the clients on both sides of the issue were not materially affected by the millions of dollars that changed hands or by the millions of dollars they had spent in legal expenses. They just moved the numbers from one column to the other on their financials. My participation in this academic exercise, however, was another matter. It came at the expense of my family, and, when all was said and done, no one cared except for my family and me.

When I arrived home at the end of the trial, I announced, "I'm home." I slumped on the couch, pouring myself a glass of wine from the bottle I'd grabbed from the kitchen. I took a sip before yelling to my husband, who was in the kids' bathroom.

"And by the way, Bob, I quit!"

With that pronouncement, the girls ran out to jump in my lap, but Bob didn't respond. Ren, Kelly, and I had a little snugglefest on the couch, and I announced to them that I would not be leaving again. They screamed and giggled, but there was still no sign of Bob.

Figuring he must not have heard me the first time, I yelled even louder.

"Bob! Are you listening? I'm never doing another trial, and I will not be away from home again for months on end!"

I waited for some resistance, an inkling of opposition . . . something. Bob still didn't respond. So, I went to find him and discovered he was on the bathroom floor with a spatula, trying to scrape up shampoo Kelly had poured out just to see what would happen. I tried, but there was no way to keep from laughing hysterically. If you've ever tried to clean up shampoo, you know that, frustratingly, everything you do just creates more bubbles. Adding to that frustration was our nanny, who had crawled out the window the night before to pursue a surfing career without giving any notice and without any surfing experience. So, we were left with no day-care options on a Monday morning. In her defense, it wasn't an entirely impulsive move, as she had consulted the expert advice of a "telepsychic" the night before she left, which we discovered a few weeks later when we received the $87 phone bill for the call.

Bob eventually broke his focus on the shampoo and looked up at me, spatula in hand. "I fully support your decision," he said decisively.

Realizing that Bob was occupied with his own situation and wasn't ignoring me, I went to fetch some paper towels to help him out. While we slowly made progress against the foamy shampoo, our girls tried enthusiastically to find something else to get into.

Bob and I spent the rest of the year analyzing our next career moves. He was also in a job that required heavy travel, and we knew that we had to make some changes. I was still not sure what I wanted to do, but I had definitely ruled out defending insurance companies and litigation from the list of possibilities. I also eliminated any area of law that required significant travel. After much analysis, I decided that my next adventure would be real estate law, which is what I had wanted to do in the first place.

Fortunately, the real estate department in the law firm I worked for was strong. I made several friends within that group, and they agreed to train me from the ground up. I took a severe cut in pay and started over in my legal career after seventeen years in litigation. While I wasn't thrilled about the pay cut, I was happy to finally be practicing the type of law that most appealed to me. My litigator friends remarked that I had just added years to my life, which might even have been the same years I'd lost during the moot court competition in law school. If my math is correct, that would mean I've broken even.

Don't get me wrong: Real estate law can have its stressful moments, but they are nothing compared to being onstage eight hours a day for five months straight. Not to mention the negativity that living in a constant state of battle-readiness can bring. Initially, litigation can sound like a lofty exchange of intellectual ideas. Later, however, the mask is lifted, and all you can hear is "did not!" and "did too!" Or, in the words made famous by Pee-wee Herman: "I know you are, but what am I?" This similarity between litigation and a class full of agitated kindergartners became apparent to me when observing actual kindergartners. But the kindergartners clearly had the edge on the trial lawyers, as they were much cuter and also much more sincere.

By this point, it was long past time to make a change. Many of my colleagues just quit law practice altogether when they reached this juncture, but I decided I had nothing to lose by trying real estate law as an alternative, and it was a good decision. For the next twenty years, I thoroughly enjoyed my real estate practice, never looking back at my decision to abandon litigation.

The work I did in real estate law involved obtaining information from clients about the project they wanted to build, then drawing up a document, outlining how the space would be shared, and drafting related documents. In my particular niche, there wasn't even an opponent, so if I could produce work that I was proud of and accomplished my clients' goals, everyone was happy. It was a considerably more serene mindset for raising children. Moreover, since I wasn't investing my entire day in cutthroat negotiations, I was more prepared to stand my ground in ceaseless negotiations with my children. Now with this new, more child-friendly career, I was ready to dive into suburbia headfirst.

CHAPTER 7

TEACH *Your* CHILDREN

FULLY EMBRACING THE SUBURBAN LIFESTYLE, we spent a lot of time on the soccer field. The games were great fun to watch, especially after we got to know the personalities of the kids and their parents. The team road trips are where the personalities really shone. On one memorable trip, a couple of the dads went out after dinner for a drink with the coach. Hours later, the team found the coach crawling up the stairs to his room. We couldn't really see how he was doing the next day, since they were playing that early morning game in a dense fog that made it hard to see the game. Whenever the girls cheered, we assumed a goal had been scored, and we faithfully cheered along with them. We could only assume that the coach was in an even heavier fog than the rest of us.

I also volunteered to drive the soccer carpool and took legal documents along to review during warmups. I usually drove the carpools in silence, listening to the chatter in the back seats. On one occasion, however, the conversation caught me completely off guard.

"Hey, Nikki. Nice slide tackle! Are those even legal in this league?" Claire asked.

"Hah, of course not," Kathryn replied.

"Alexa, has your dad recovered from the red card he got at the game last weekend?" Olivia jumped in. "Oh my God, that was so funny when the ref threw him out. Just for a little f-bomb over a crappy penalty call!"

This prompted Angela to respond from the back: "Right, but your mom almost got ejected after she took a piece out of that parent on the other team who literally did a drum roll every time his team scored."

"I know!" said Ren. "Who even brings a drum set to a soccer game?"

Their voices suddenly lowered to a whisper as I struggled to overhear.

"Did you guys hear that Sonia is pregnant?" asked Angela.

My eyes widened as I took a sip of my coffee.

"No! What's she going to do?" Alexa asked, shocked.

"She's excited, and she's going to have the baby," Angela informed them.

"But she's thirteen!" Alexa squealed.

No longer able to contain myself, I choked and sprayed latte all over the dashboard. We had a family chat about teen pregnancy that evening, spewing out all the precautions that we could think of to set both of our girls straight on this issue. In the middle of our discussion, one of our daughters asked sincerely: "But if we did get pregnant, you would raise the baby, right?"

Bob and I blurted out, almost in unison: "*Absolutely not!* We were old when we had you, and we are definitely too old to start over."

The question made us concerned that they may have missed the point of our lecture about caution and responsibility, so we went through it one more time to be sure we had been clear. There was a lot of eye-rolling around the table, but we persevered.

During fake business meetings and conference calls I contrived to excuse my absence from the office, I attended track and cross-country meets, softball games, and volleyball and basketball games; volunteered as a co-op Brownie mom; and drove the kids on field trips. To this point, two of the best days of my life were the day that my girls quit Brownies and the day they quit softball. It turned out that while the Brownie troops had some normal moms, they also had a couple of, let's just say, "moms from hell." One mom actually said out loud during a meeting, "Well, you *work*, so you obviously don't care about your child."

I walked out on that meeting with the support of a stay-at-home mom who had been just as offended as I was by the remark. It turned out that the mom who'd said that to me had been fired from her job by her own father the week before, so she may have had some issues regarding working moms that were entirely unrelated to me.

Then there was softball, which could involve hours of watching a game in a cold rain while your child picked daisies in the outfield. Kelly was quite good at the daisy picking, but she couldn't have cared less about the sport. While she may not have had a passion for the actual game, she did enjoy the snacks. Before every game, we bought her a packet of sunflower seeds so she could stand around in the dugout, spitting out the shells like a pro. Eventually, some parents ran afoul of the no-alcohol rules and began to bring libations in thermoses, just to weather the cold and rain. Our conversations usually revolved around whether the coach had played our marginally-talented children enough to justify our braving the elements to watch the games. The girls' skills seemed to improve over the time they spent in the under-ten group, since at that stage, there was a parent pitcher who usually threw the pitch somewhere near the plate. Once they turned ten, however, we were back to square one, because the girls were just learning to pitch for themselves. A wild pitch was the norm during those games. I remember one time, Bob had grown impatient, announcing, "We're on a run of eighteen balls and no strikes. Hey, Carol, can you hand me that thermos?"

I wasn't the only one in the house who juggled home life and work. When our daughters were growing up, Bob had a demanding job as a CEO in the electronics industry. Of course, we were exhausted every day of our lives, balancing family and careers as best we could. Given the competing demands on our time, the time we donated to schools and teams all had to involve direct contact with our kids. We didn't have time to keep the books for the softball team, but we decided we could work the concession stand, scooping up globs of melted orange "cheese" onto defenseless nachos and chili dogs for the anxiously waiting children. After my first stint as the nacho lady, trying to stir a vat of the gelatinous substance into a liquid, I vowed never to eat nachos again.

Despite Bob's schedule, he never missed a sports event, an open house, a science fair, or a parent-teacher conference. He was also in charge of making breakfast for the girls and handled it in exactly the manner you would expect of someone with an engineering background and an MBA from Stanford: He learned how to make four things. Every Monday he served hot cereal, Tuesday was scrambled eggs (green eggs and ham when the girls were little), Wednesday was pancakes (in the shape of Minnie Mouse, of course), Thursday was omelets, and Friday was cold cereal. The girls' teachers knew which day was omelet day and occasionally offered to come by and join us for breakfast. We never took them up on the offer, since that would have been awkward, but Bob was flattered that they all knew the schedule and expressed an interest in the healthy fare that he was preparing for our kids. The breakfast schedule never changed until the girls graduated high school.

I was thrilled that Bob had taken his responsibilities for morning duty so seriously. I credit him for contributing to both of our daughters' passion for healthy food later in life. When visiting during school breaks, they would meticulously check the expiration date of everything in our pantry and fridge and toss anything that had expired. They would also critique the remainder of our food and teach us how to make our diet healthier. It was clear even then that the tables were turning. Instead of us teaching them, well, they were teaching us.

CHAPTER 8

THE TIMES *They* ARE A-CHANGIN'

AS NEIGHBORS, JENNY AND I were often a great source of support and comfort to one another. I remember 9/11, when we sat together on my front doorstep, crying and trying to figure out how our world had just changed. We didn't know if we would ever fly on a commercial airline again, or if we would be hit by an attack of bioterrorism or chemical warfare. The round-the-clock news assured us that anything was possible and laid out scenarios that neither of us could process. We worried whether any of our children would reach adulthood. We sat there and strategized, between bouts of tears, about how to share the news with our kids.

At the time, Jenny's daughters and son were still in elementary school, and my daughters were in second grade and kindergarten. After a few hours and cups of coffee, we dreamed up some platitudes to break the news to our children gently. We were still perfecting the presentation when my kindergartner was dropped off and screamed as she ran into the house, "Mom, did you hear that some guys crashed a plane into a big building and killed everybody?"

The only time we laughed that day was at our naïveté in thinking that our children were in a bubble while at school. It must have been obvious to everyone except us that news spreads faster through a playground than anywhere else. It was moments like these that created a lasting bond between us, which came in handy whenever life threw us a few curves.

One such curve came when both of my girls were in high school. During these years, there was a lot going on with our daughters, who had thankfully narrowed their participation in sports to track, cross-country, soccer, swimming, and volleyball. There also were driving lessons, SATs, college applications and tours, and "teenage activities," many of which are best forgotten but are, in fact, indelibly etched on our minds. The worst ones will never see print and are too painful to even discuss, but there are a couple I can mention.

In high school, we grounded Ren for something we don't even remember at this point. Bob and I were downstairs and couldn't hear the sound of footsteps on the creaky wooden floors above us, which we thought was odd. After a while, we went up and knocked. But there was no answer. So, we knocked again—nothing. We then opened the door and found the window wide open in the dead of winter. With the benefit of our forensic skills, we deduced that Ren had hopped out of the second-story window, onto a friend's car, and taken off. We had thought Ren's aptitude in sports would keep her on the straight and narrow, but all it had done was make it easier for her to sneak out of our house by jumping out of a second-story window.

The other teenage activity is less creative but much more common. The beauty, however, is in the execution. In my day, when we cut class, we simply presented a carefully forged excuse to the office. At some point, my siblings and I realized that the office had four signatures on file: our three forged signatures plus our mom's real signature. We had gales of laughter over that one. Schools have since caught on to this, so when our kids were in high school, we received a phone message most evenings at precisely 7:00 p.m. while we were having dinner. We got the call so often that we can quote it even now: "This is the attendance office of Aragon High School. We are calling to inform you that your child, [fill in the name], has missed one or more classes today. If this was an excused absence, please send a note with your child to the office tomorrow. Otherwise, the absence will be considered a truancy."

Of course, it was never an excused absence or we would have sent a note in the first place. So, we would question the truant of the day as to what had happened. Typically, there was a substitute who didn't recognize them and confused them with another student. After that explanation had worn thin, it was the teacher who was so stupid that they didn't even know how to take roll and skipped over them even though they were sitting right in front of the teacher the whole time. The last resort was that they had [insert random excuse: a headache, cramps, a stomachache, a bad hair day] and just missed that class while sitting outside to restore their mental or physical health. At this stage, you begin to wonder if your kids really think that (a) you were never a teenager; (b) you never tried the same tricks; and (c) you are actually clueless enough to believe any of their excuses.

It got to the point that when the phone rang at 7:00, one of us would pick it up, and we would all say in unison: "This is the attendance office . . ." As long as their grades didn't suffer and they were still attending enough classes to graduate, we didn't worry too much that they were skipping ceramics or whatever the class du jour was. Of course, we chastised them and offered astute lectures on the value of education, but they fell on deaf ears, so we learned to pick our battles.

In that era, I was immersed in real estate law, with most of my work generated by my boss, Leslie, who was a hard-driving marketing genius. She had a large Energizer Bunny in her office. No one needed to ask why. By all appearances, Leslie required no sleep. She treated each of her clients like royalty, cranking out their work in record time, with the help of her minions, such as myself. She would gleefully hand out a four-hour project and announce that she had promised it to the client within half an hour. As you can imagine, not everyone survived this stress-inducing environment.

In her spare time (at 3:00 or 4:00 a.m.), Leslie baked scones and other delicacies to bring to the office. She also kept a garden of sweet peas, which she used to decorate her secretaries' desks. Yes, she had more than one secretary, since one was not enough to keep up with her frenetic pace. She had a constitution made of steel and never got sick. At one point, she had a bunionectomy and was hopping around the office in a boot the very next day. This made it difficult for her to understand why anyone would need downtime for any type of medical procedure.

During this time, I went through my most momentous pre-cancer medical scare, and Jenny quite literally supported me, helping me walk around the block until I was able to do so on my own. I was in my early fifties and had had a hysterectomy that went horribly wrong. Shortly prior to the hysterectomy, I had been hospitalized with twisted intestines. Many of our friends commented that their dogs or even horses had experienced this but that, they had never encountered another human being who had endured this affliction and to date, neither have I.

In any case, I was just about to be released from the emergency room where I had been sent by my primary care physician for abdominal pain—most likely with a parenthetical note of "hypochondria" at the bottom of my hospital chart—when a surgeon, Dr. Clark, took a second look at the scan and noticed the twist in my intestines. This required me to stay in the hospital for observation. If the situation didn't resolve itself, surgery would be required. He and I chatted about this condition and derided those who had dismissed my complaints as indigestion or heartburn. We forged a friendship, which we both assumed would only last for the three days I was hospitalized for observation. Fortunately, during that time my intestines untwisted, so I was sent on my way.

However, two weeks later I had a previously scheduled laparoscopic hysterectomy. Like many women my age, I had developed fibroid tumors—cumulatively about the size of a grapefruit—with the unfortunate result that I had my period nonstop for more than a year. Many procedures had been done to address the bleeding, including D&Cs and an endometrial ablation. My doctor, Dr. Cole, finally decided that we had reached the end of the road with minimally invasive procedures, and we needed to go forward with the hysterectomy. She initially suggested that we follow the traditional method of major abdominal surgery, which required at least six weeks of recovery time. I knew that Leslie would have no patience for this, and it was a busy time in the real estate industry, so I opted for the laparoscopic procedure.

A laparoscopic hysterectomy is just a fancy way of saying that the whole procedure is done by putting a tiny camera into a few small incisions in your abdomen and hauling out your uterus through your belly button. It is much less invasive than a longer slice through your abdomen, and it has a much shorter recovery time—one or two weeks instead of six. I explained to Dr. Cole that this was the only option for me, since I could only afford to take a couple of weeks off work. Unfortunately, I forgot to ask if she'd ever done the laparoscopic procedure before, and she forgot to mention that she hadn't.

Post-surgery, she was proud. She popped into the recovery room and announced confidently that everything had gone great. Bob was relieved to hear the news and immediately emailed Leslie to report that I had come through the surgery like a champ. Over the next few hours, though, it became apparent that things were not actually going all that well. I felt like crap in a way that I couldn't yet describe, so the doctors decided to keep me in the hospital for an extra day. In the middle of the night, I pushed the button to call a nurse to my room. I could hear talking and laughter from the nurses' station, but no one responded. I pushed the button again; nothing. Finally, in desperation, I picked up a water bottle and threw it out the door to get their attention. Within seconds, a nurse appeared in my room.

"I don't think I'm supposed to be in this much pain," I explained in a pathetically weak voice. On the one to ten pain chart that shows ten as the agonized face with tears running down it as the worst pain possible, I was undoubtedly a ten. In case I wasn't clear, I told them, "I've had a couple of surgeries before, and I know that this is not surgical pain. This is intestinal pain, and it's a freaking ten on the chart. Can you please call Dr. Clark, who treated me for an intestinal issue two weeks ago?"

I'm certain this caused more laughter at the nurses' station. I can just hear them now: "Call a surgeon in the middle of the night for a whining patient? I don't think so." In any event, he wasn't called. As an act of mercy or to silence me until the day shift took over, they upped my morphine. I appreciated the gesture, but in the morning I was considerably worse. Finally, at 6:00 a.m., Dr. Clark came in. Almost as soon as he crossed the threshold to my room, he ran back out.

Later, he apologized for this mysterious behavior, explaining, "As soon as I saw you, I ran out to schedule the operating room. You had about an hour left."

Have you ever wondered or been asked the question, "What would you do if you knew you only had six months left to live?"

Six months seems relatively short in the scheme of things, so most of us respond that we would quit work, spend time with our families, spend all our money and travel, or something to that effect. But what if you only had an hour? That's barely enough time to send in the resignation letter, much less book a flight.

Right before they wheeled me back into the operating room, Bob called. He was getting our daughters ready to come over and visit, but it would still be another hour or two before they all could get there. I suggested, in my still pathetically weak voice, in a way that left no room for argument, that he change those plans, however, and have the girls fend for themselves for a few hours, because he needed to get his ass over to the hospital right away.

Turns out during the hysterectomy my intestines were punctured, resulting in an emergency bowel resection, massive infections, pneumonia, pleurisy, a collapsed lung, and a twenty-four-day hospitalization. For a couple of days after the emergency intestinal surgery, I was so drugged that I was hallucinating. I was convinced that one of the nurses had assaulted me, which never actually happened. When I tried to sleep, I felt as though my bed were vertical and I was about to fall out of it. This bizarre feeling lasted for hours, though apparently my bed was never actually vertical. Even the 1960s and 1970s had not prepared me for this type of experience.

I was out of commission for so long that my hairdresser actually stopped by the hospital to color my roots. Other friends offered to bring colored tennis balls for my walker. And Bob and I spent innumerable hours strolling the hallways of the hospital with all my IVs in tow. Leslie called once a week or so to ask when I would be returning to work. Had I not known her reputation for perseverance at all costs, this might have put me off. In any event, I was too weak to care, so I just promised to be back in touch with her once I left the hospital.

One of my other law partners, Derek, who had just written a book titled *Images of Death*, offered me a free copy. He'd had a life-threatening experience with prostate cancer and since then had volunteered at a hospice and wrote regular blogs on each patient that he attended to. I guess you could say he had a little bit of an obsession with death. When he offered to come visit me in the hospital, I was mortified. Did I really want one of my male law partners to see me in a hospital gown, so bloated that I looked about seven months pregnant? Not to mention the whole death theme, which I really didn't want to dwell on for very long, given my current physical state. So, I solicited one of my other partners to persuade him to stay away.

Dr. Clark and I cemented our friendship during my stay, until I busted him for sneaking out to smoke cigarettes before his rounds at 6:00 a.m. Even that called for a good laugh, since he was certain that he had disguised the smell with cologne and mints. During our conversations, I learned that most of the people who die from gunshot wounds actually die from perforated intestines, like I had suffered at the inexperienced hands of my surgeon.

Much to my daughter Ren's credit, when Dr. Cole, who had botched the surgery, came in to apologize to Bob and the kids, which is what hospitals recommend these days to thwart off any hostile feelings that might result in lawsuits, she stared back at the doctor, cold-faced. When Dr. Cole left the room, Ren said, "I know she wanted me to say it's okay, but it's not. She almost killed you, and I can't say that's okay just to make her feel better." My girls were already tremendous champions for my cause. Neither one suffers from my aversion to confrontation.

I lost twenty-five pounds during my three-and-a-half-week hospital stay. And by the time I was discharged, I looked like a walking skeleton. Since the hysterectomy, I've had an additional fourteen surgeries. Most were orthopedic surgeries and may have been caused by "unspecified connective tissue disorder." Every year or so, another tendon or ligament gave way for no apparent reason and required repair. I also had fibromyalgia, which can be a side effect of physical trauma (such as my near-death experience), and I had arthritis in virtually every joint. The combination of these painful conditions muddied the waters and made it difficult to determine the source of the pain. My formerly invincible self became strangely vulnerable in mysterious ways.

Bob can attest to the fact that surgery has become so routine in my life that we simply do a "drive by" for my procedures. At my insistence, Bob drops me off at the hospital, without noticeably slowing down. Then I hop out, and the nurses call him when I'm done. We are the model of efficiency when it comes to medical procedures.

Because I have had more than my share of torn tendons, ligaments, and other orthopedic issues, all of which have occurred in the absence of any external injury, I have spent way too much time hoping to obtain clarity on the cause or interrelationship of these issues, ending in frustration at the lack of answers or even working theories. I started with what I will call the circuit of doctors, where the first doesn't have a clue, so they refer you to a specialist. The specialist is stumped, so they send you to another specialist, and they each order legions of tests along the way. The tests give the doctors other issues to explore, even though those issues were not the reason for the visit. Eventually, you end up back at the first doctor, no more enlightened as to the nature of the condition than on the initial visit. Eventually, I gave up on the medical profession and started grilling my friends as to whether they had heard of similar situations. It was not long before I'd shared so much with friends about my injuries and surgeries that those who had not already left the room during my conversations and inquiries probably wished they had.

Having exhausted my doctors and social contacts, I resorted to Internet research. I consider myself the reigning queen of the medical Internet, with more than one app on my phone to match up symptoms with a diagnosis. Medicine.net is especially fun, because you can start with one symptom, get a thousand options, then keep adding symptoms to narrow the field. In minutes, I can make a self-diagnosis, when the highly trained doctors who are running me in circles don't have a clue. Of course, my diagnoses are always wrong, but that doesn't deter me from my research.

CHAPTER 9

THERE'S GOLD *in* *Them* THAR HILLS!

THE YEAR THAT KELLY GRADUATED from high school, a flyer promoting a golf and lake community at Lake Tahoe arrived in the mail. Bob and I were cordially invited to witness firsthand everything this community had to offer over the Fourth of July weekend, courtesy of the community's sales team. While we couldn't resist an all-expense-paid trip, we couldn't have cared less about the community. Bob and I were not above sitting in on a ninety-minute sales pitch in exchange for being courted and pampered by the sales team for a few days. As seasoned veterans of the real estate industry, we felt invulnerable to even the most polished sales pitch, so we decided to pack our bags and take them up on their offer.

Given my track record of making momentous decisions in mere seconds, like when I had purchased my first home, we made a firm pact on the way to the mountains that we were *not buying* a home at Lake Tahoe. We were just enjoying the weekend. However, by the time we embarked on this trek, both of our kids were off to college, Bob was retired, and my employer didn't care if I worked "from the moon," so we were a tad more vulnerable than we gave ourselves credit for.

Upon our arrival, the low-key sales team, headed up by Nick, greeted us at the pool. In retrospect, the low-key aspect may have disarmed us a bit. We graciously accepted the offer of a beer. Nick then asked if we needed anything else and pointed out his office just across the street. Bob engaged in some sales banter with the guy and jokingly quipped, "Just a tequila chaser, ha, ha."

Of course, shots of tequila miraculously appeared soon after, and our resolve started to slip away. Then Nick extended another friendly offer.

"Oh, by the way, we're taking a group to the lake tomorrow night for fireworks. Do you want to come along?"

We both nodded. "Sure, that sounds like fun."

Nick smiled and shook our hands, encouraging us to enjoy our time at the pool. After he left, we carefully laid our towels out on the cement, since all the lounge chairs were occupied, and sipped our drinks while we took in the breathtaking views. I already imagined myself living here, having lunch and cocktails delivered to me by the pool. I was still working, so of course my new office would be poolside. I could start the day in the gym, do some work, play some golf or ski, then finish my work for the day at the pool. In the shoulder seasons (April to June and September to December), I could work like a dog in perfect peace up in the mountains and make up for the goofing off that I planned to do during the summer and winter months. I could get used to this, but our pact in the car precluded me from going too far down this road.

The next day we attended the requisite ninety-minute session with the sales team, which quickly turned into a four-hour tour of every available lot. After the tour, we headed back to the pool to spend the afternoon, where Bob started working on what appeared to be a cash-flow analysis. Bob's idea of a good time is playing with numbers, so I didn't give this much thought. In fact, I never ask him why he is calculating anything, for fear he may tell me. I can't even pretend to be interested in calculations. The low point in my college career was nearly failing Economics 101. I thought, as a veteran shopper, that I understood the whole supply-and-demand concept, but on the midterm I apparently drew all the curves demonstrating those concepts upside down. I went into the final with a failing grade but somehow managed to eke out a C– in the class. Needless to say, I have not taken a math, finance, or economics class since.

After a relaxing afternoon at the pool—for me, at least—we went off to the lake for the fireworks. There was an area roped off for the community right on the lake at Jake's, a well-known restaurant in the area. The restaurant provided dinner, and the wine was flowing. Fireworks over the lake were spectacular. On the way back from the lake, while we were sitting in the back of the bus, we all shared a bottle of bourbon to pass the time while we waited out the lake traffic. This is when the relationships were solidified. The whole excursion to the lake for fireworks may have been a carefully staged setup courtesy of the sales team, but we didn't care. We were having fun, and we were *not* buying.

The following day we played golf. Even with our hangovers and botched swings, we were able to enjoy the beautiful course with breathtaking views of the Carson Range from the back nine. We played most of the game in relative silence, since we were still recovering from the Fourth of July festivities from the previous night.

We basked in the warm weather, having become accustomed to playing golf in the swirling fog of the Bay Area, and noted how we never had to wait on others during the entire round. We couldn't recall a round of golf in the recent past where we had not become impatient waiting for some guy to finish smoking his cigar on the green and move on. There were also the gamblers who took a good five minutes to evaluate every putt before pulling the trigger, lest they lose their dignity and twenty bucks to the other guys. So, all in all, regardless of our scores, we were relaxed and enjoyed our time on the course. When I lost three balls in the water on the eighteenth hole, there was a slight risk our peaceful afternoon would be shattered, but even a double-digit score on the last hole didn't put a damper on that gorgeous day we had in the mountains. At the end of the game, Bob suggested that we stop by the sales office, just to say goodbye and to thank our gracious hosts. After all, it was the polite thing to do.

When we got to the sales office, Nick was there, along with other members of the sales team.

"Hey, guys, how was the weekend?" Nick greeted us.

"It was great," Bob said. "We met some fun people, had a nice round of golf, and enjoyed the tour yesterday. Thanks for everything. Your whole team was really very accommodating. You seem to have a great community in the making here. Now, we just need to get back on the road and brave the traffic to get home."

"So glad you enjoyed it," Nick said. "Were there any lots or townhomes that you saw yesterday that may have sparked an interest?"

"Actually, there was one," Bob replied, "but we're not in a position to make an offer, and, even if we were, we don't know if we would want one of the furnished townhomes or a lot where we could build a custom home."

I realized then that Bob was considering making an offer and started holding my breath. The cash-flow analysis was starting to crinkle in his back pocket. We hadn't said a word about making an offer over the weekend, not even on the golf course, where we were by ourselves for a few hours. Nevertheless, Bob must have sensed the emotional pull that a home in Tahoe had for me, so he forged ahead without so much as a glance in my direction.

"What would the down payment be on the lot? And what about the model townhome? We like the fact that it's fully furnished, ready to occupy."

Bob was asking dozens of specific questions at a rapid clip. None of those questions conveyed the message that we were *not buying*.

"Do you think the developer would agree to change the fireplace in the townhome," I asked. We didn't really like the stone that had been used. *Oops*, I wondered. *Did I jump too far ahead in the process here? Maybe I should just sit tight for a while.*

"Would you live here full time or use it as a second home?" asked Jamie, another member of the sales team.

"No, no, no," Bob responded, "we're just daydreaming. We don't want to mislead you into thinking that we can make an offer."

"Oh yeah, you were asking *if*," Nick emphasized.

"As long as you know that this is a *hypothetical* conversation we're having," Bob said carefully, "because, again, we are *not* considering buying anything, I'd say it would have to be full time. We can't support two homes."

"If you were here full time, you'd probably want to build a home with the right amount of space," Nick explained.

"Hmm, okay," Bob replied. "Well, if we did make an offer on anything today, how much time would we have to back out?"

"You can have thirty days with no commitment whatsoever."

Bob nodded. "Okay, then as long as you don't mind wasting your time with us, we can at least write up an offer. In fact, we can do one for the lot that we liked and the other for the townhome, since we're not likely to go through with either one."

Was Bob talking out of both sides of his mouth? I was trying to listen, but at this point I couldn't tell whether he was truly interested or just playing with these guys. As we were writing up the offers, the developer stopped by. He offered us a couple of final concessions to entice us to sign. He seemed like a nice guy, closely involved with the community.

By this time, I risked lapsing into unconsciousness from holding my breath. Having committed early on to sitting tight during the discussion, I was uncharacteristically silent during the negotiation, except to offer a couple of comments on the conditions in the offers. I was afraid if I said a word, the spell would be broken. Meanwhile, my mind was racing. *We could be building a home? We could live in a place that we designed according to our taste and to suit our lifestyle? Argh! Living on a golf course, near the lake?* At this point, I alternated between holding my breath and hyperventilating. *Or we could buy that model townhome and be living up here in a matter of weeks.* I was taking mental inventory of our Bay Area home, deciding which furniture would suit a mountain environment and which wouldn't. In my mind, I was already selecting lighting and finishes for the custom home option. It's possible I was jumping the gun, but as long as I kept these thoughts to myself, no one could put a damper on my euphoria.

Four hours later, we left the resort with an offer on a vacant lot *and* an offer on a model townhome, fully furnished down to the placemats. Over the next thirty days, we would decide which one made more sense for the purchase we were "not going to make." As we headed back home, I still didn't believe for a second that we would go through with it. I thought it was just a fun thought exercise for the two of us, and we would soon reject it for being ill-conceived, impulsive, too expensive, or just outright impractical. As long as no one else knew about it, there was no finality. Then, on the way home that Sunday, we called our youngest daughter, Kelly. I thought we were just checking in to see how the weekend was going when suddenly Bob blurted out, "Guess what we just bought?!"

Kelly remarked that this was the first impulsive thing he had ever done. I sat with a silly grin on my face for the rest of the ride home. As soon as we got home, we showed her the brochures. She jumped right in and started planning out her bedroom, dreaming of weekends with twenty or so of her closest friends and a fully stocked refrigerator. Presumably, we would be asked to relocate for these weekends. We called our other daughter, Ren, and asked how she felt about us moving to the mountains. She replied without hesitation: "I do not see any scenario where I will *ever* again live in the suburbs." She had no intention of becoming the boomerang child, moving back home after college.

Now that others were in on the deal, I finally believed that it might really happen. Nevertheless, Bob remained concerned that the move might be financially unwise. The cash-flow analysis was becoming dog-eared as we contemplated our options. In my mind, the move felt right, and finances never dominated my thoughts. Lake Tahoe had special meaning for our family. Bob and I had met there, we had spent almost every Christmas there when our daughters were growing up, and we spent one week every summer at a family camp at a nearby lake. I was drawn to the mountains and the lake and to a lifestyle focused around outdoor sports.

Bob did some more math and concluded that we could rent our San Mateo home for an amount that would pay the mortgage on our current home *as well* as the new home. It turned out that a move to the mountains wouldn't be an extravagance after all, because the rental market in the Bay Area had gone through the roof. Wasn't this the type of opportunity we had saved up for our entire lives? A little more of Bob's math led to the conclusion that— if we watched our budget—we could even build our own home for the cost of purchasing the fully furnished townhome. Once the deal made financial sense to Bob, he was on board.

In early September, we closed escrow on the lot. Patience is not my virtue, so building a house was difficult for me. The usual time frame for construction was nothing but slow torture. We were rapidly closing in on the deadline for pouring a foundation in Tahoe, normally October fifteenth, since the ground was starting to freeze. I knew I could not wait an additional year to start construction, so we had to devise some way to start building before the winter. We adapted an existing plan from an architect who had built other homes in the community, making a few changes to suit our taste. We got lucky, and that year there was no snow in October, so the deadline for pouring a foundation was extended to November first. We rushed through all the necessary approvals, and the foundation was miraculously poured just before the extended deadline.

Shortly after we made the offer, I had begun to select bedding, towels, bathmats, fixtures, finishes, and lighting. I developed my "home in a bag" concept, where I schlepped a canvas bag from one store to the next, building color schemes for each bedroom and bath along the way. Later in the process, I chose the tile, flooring, paint colors, and trim. Choosing my own tiles ranked up there as one of my top-ten life shopping experiences. We all handle empty nesting differently. Apparently, my coping mechanism was choosing tile.

During this time, Bob worked closely with the contractor to answer any questions that might delay construction and made regular trips to Tahoe to monitor progress and compliance with the architectural plans. Of course, there were a few hiccups along the way, which always happens during construction. However, it wasn't in Bob's nature to let any detail slide just to accommodate the contractor. When the contractor showed Bob the "great-looking" fire pit, we thought it looked as if it came from the Flintstone era. Bob said bluntly, "Rip it out. It's ugly." So, it was quickly demolished and replaced with a much nicer fire pit, which somehow became the new standard for other homes in the community.

Bob and I knew better than to ask our contractor for a completion estimate. We assumed that any estimate would be a white lie, subject to change for little or no reason. Therefore, we made a conscious decision to rise above this dynamic and never asked when the house would be done until about March, six months after construction started. Perhaps we were too generous with the timeline.

That winter came in the midst of a severe drought in California, and the result had been no snow and no snow delays. Construction had sailed through at a breakneck pace, so by the time we finally summoned our courage to ask our contractor for a completion estimate, he said that due to the snowless winter, our home was ahead of schedule and would be done sometime in May—much sooner than we had anticipated. We rushed to schedule our move for June so we could spend the summer at Lake Tahoe!

PART THREE:

The News

CHAPTER 10

The WOMEN'S CENTER

IT WAS OFFICIAL: CONSTRUCTION WAS finished, and we were moving to our dream home in Lake Tahoe the next day. There were hundreds of little moving and packing details to attend to, but because of Jenny's insistence at our goodbye luncheon a couple of weeks prior, one of them was dutifully showing up at the Women's Center at Mills Hospital to have a 3-D mammogram. Other than the annoyance of having to take time out of my busy schedule, it wasn't a big deal. Just one more item to check off my to-do list.

The logistics of moving and packing cluttered every corner of my mind. After I checked in at the Women's Center, I continued to pore over countless details of the next day's move: *Have I labeled everything right? Where is everything going in the new house? Do I know where my clothes are for tomorrow? Did I put the right furniture in storage? Will I be able to stay awake long enough to drive up to Tahoe after the movers finish packing?*

After checking in at the main reception desk, I was led to the changing area, which doubled as a waiting room. There, I donned one of the trendy hospital gowns. I read the usual cautionary signs asking if I had any lotions on or had used deodorant that day. I hadn't even had time to *think* about those things, much less apply them. Moreover, there was no chance of finding lotions or deodorant in the packing disaster that was our home. As I sat there, I watched the anxious women in the waiting room awaiting their results. I didn't feel any connection to them. I was healthy. I worked out almost daily and ate a predominately healthy diet. In my mind, I was invincible. Besides, I was just here to appease Jenny. Pretty soon I'd be done with this formality and get back to packing.

While I was waiting, I looked up from my phone and noticed one woman who had been called back after her mammogram for an ultrasound. She had brought a friend with her who was lovingly holding her hand. They talked lightheartedly about everything but breast cancer. Eventually, the woman was called into the hallway and given the all clear by the technician. I watched as the woman's face softened with relief as she and her friend did a little victory dance.

I vicariously enjoyed their moment, trying to imagine what it would be like to feel the vulnerability of more testing and then to have the confirmation that everything was okay. I looked around the waiting room and noticed that all the other women were smiling at her obvious relief too. I returned to my phone to catch up on emails, which were coming in at the speed of light. It seemed that whenever I needed to take personal time for something like a move or medical appointment, the pace of work accelerated.

"Mrs. Croshaw," I heard my name called from the hallway. I stood up and grabbed my purse. *Great, now it's my turn. Let's get this show on the road. I still need to pack up the fridge.*

As I met the mammogram tech in the doorway, she smiled. "And how are you doing today?" I wondered how many of these she had already done today and how long this was going to take. She was middle-aged, like me, and had curled her blond hair. I noticed that she had the calming demeanor of an experienced medical professional. I was certain that her experience meant she would be efficient and move this process along. I also thought her experience would lessen the chance of a false positive, which I understood to be one of the risks of the 3-D equipment. I actually had done a little Internet research on the procedure after my lunch with Jenny.

"I'm doing really well, thank you," I said. "We're moving tomorrow, and I'm so excited I could wet my pants."

The woman laughed. "That's wonderful. Where are you moving to?"

"Lake Tahoe."

"Wow, I hear it's beautiful up there."

"Yup, that's why we chose it."

As I followed her down the hall, I noticed the pictures on the wall, mostly landscapes, which I'm certain were intended to be a calming distraction. We walked down the remainder of the long corridor in awkward silence. Then we took a right turn down a second long corridor. We kept walking, passing the radiologist, whom I recognized from prior visits, and a few other women headed for their mammograms and ultrasounds. When we got about halfway down that hallway, she stopped and motioned toward the imaging room, indicating that was where we would do the mammogram.

After I entered the imaging room, the technician asked me some questions, including "Have you ever had an ultrasound of your breasts? Do you have any implants? Have you had prior breast surgery? Are you aware of any lumps?"

Before she could even finish a question, I was already spitting out the answer, just to keep the process moving so I could get out of there. As the question-and-answer session progressed, I studied her.

"You look familiar. How long have you been here?" I asked.

She smiled. "About twenty-five years."

"Well, that explains it. We probably met on one of my other visits."

The woman nodded. "That could be."

She then started with the mammogram. Initially, nothing was out of the ordinary. And it turned out, I had remembered this tech from a prior visit. She was a pro, mixing just the right amount of chitchat with the business at hand to keep me distracted from the fact that my boobs were being flattened like pancakes.

As she positioned me a little closer to the machine, she apologized, "Sorry, this may be a little uncomfortable."

I winced from the pinch. *No kidding.*

"So, how long have you lived here?" she asked, deflecting my attention.

I let out a deep breath, trying to at least pretend that I was comfortable. "About eighteen years."

The woman walked back to a computer in the back so she could start taking images.

"Do you have any children?" she continued.

I nodded. "Yes, two girls. One is in college, and the other is starting college in the fall."

The tech told me to hold my breath while she took the images. Between shots I asked her if she had ever heard the joke about a mammogram being similar to lying on the floor of a cold garage and having a car drive over your boobs. She shook her head. Hard to believe, but she hadn't.

After my joke fell flat, we were silent for a moment. She helped turn me to get the next set of images. "Now we'll do the other side, and then we'll be done."

I was relieved to get another item off my checklist. Soon I'd be back at home and could clean out that fridge.

"Looks like we're all finished," she announced with a perky lilt to her voice. "If you could wait here for just a few minutes, we'll have the radiologist take a quick look and make sure the pictures are good."

I nodded and resumed my litany of thoughts about packing and everything that I still needed to do before tomorrow's move. I distracted myself with a few games of Sudoku on my phone and made lists of things I needed to do when I got home. Ten or fifteen minutes later, the tech returned, and thinking back to it now, she was not as chipper as she'd been when she left the room before. That should have been a big clue right there, but I was too focused on packing to notice anything short of a car driving over my boobs.

Then she said something that should have rung out like a gunshot in the room: "We didn't get a good picture of the left side, so we need to try that again." It should have occurred to me that the tech had done literally **hundreds**, if not **thousands,** of mammograms. It wasn't her first rodeo, and she certainly knew a good picture from a bad one before she even took it to the radiologist. Surely there must have been times when they really *didn't* get a good picture, maybe with a less-experienced tech, but in the moment I underestimated the possibility that she was simply taking a diplomatic approach to saying, "The radiologist saw something, and we need to get a better look at it." I shook off that option immediately. Our impending move could not share center stage in my thoughts.

I didn't really have the time or the inclination to entertain anything else, excluding a few interruptions from my office with things that just couldn't wait. Under normal circumstances, I might have focused or even obsessed on the tech taking a second picture during the mammogram, but I had enough going on to prevent my mind from wandering off in that direction.

There was a time in my life when I expected a disaster at least every six months. I realized that if six months went by without the sky falling, I would become anxious waiting for the next blow. I was over that by now, having gained the confidence that I did deserve the good things that came my way and didn't need to hedge my bets with the idea that every action has an equal and opposite reaction in life just as it does in physics. I was not going to ruin or even dilute the positive moments in my life with such negative thoughts. Little did I know that soon I would have to reopen the door to the negativity chamber and make room for other issues—lots of them.

CHAPTER 11

LEAVING *the* 'BURBS

AFTER LEAVING THE IMAGING CENTER, I could finally get back to packing. I was very excited about everything that the move signified. It represented a significant change in our life-style, and I am a firm believer in shaking things up from time to time. We had never lived in a small town, nor had we lived in the mountains or in a place where it snows. We'd never built a home, so Bob and I were looking forward to the change and the newness of everything.

We were making good progress on the packing, carefully labeling each box by destination and contents. There was no room for error. As a joke, I stuck some tape on my forehead labeled "Master Bedroom" so no one would leave me behind and I would be sent to the appropriate location upon our late-night arrival. Bob had suffered through twenty-plus years of my antics and so was only mildly amused. Given the stress a moving day brings, I was content with "mildly amused."

Moving day

The movers finally arrived and started packing the van. As they were loading up, however, my cell phone rang. I answered and heard someone ask, "Is this Cathy? This is the Women's Center, calling about your mammogram. We'd like to schedule you to come back in for an ultrasound."

The nagging thought about why they needed a second picture for the mammogram was still only lurking in the back of my mind. Consciously, I thought, *Jeez, I actually did have one of those false positives, so I have to go back and waste more time just to be told that there's nothing wrong. They couldn't have picked a worse time to annoy me.* The movers would be done loading in just a few hours, so I offered, "Fine, does now work? The moving van is here, and I'll be gone as soon as we're packed up." I didn't think they would be able to accommodate me so soon, but when they agreed, I started to wonder if maybe something *was* wrong. I now know that when anyone in the medical profession is *that* accommodating, worrying is warranted.

Determined to get it over with, I trundled back on down to the Women's Center and headed into the reception area, where I was once again shown into the changing room. This time I was the one beginning to look a little unsettled, not to mention annoyed. After I'd played ten rounds of Candy Crush on my phone, someone called my name.

I followed the technician into an adjacent room. By now, I was actually enjoying a breather from the moving activities, since the movers were currently packing the truck and my job was basically done. While I was waiting for the ultrasound to start, I checked in on the emails from my office and made multiple lists to keep me on track for the next few days. I outlined everything that had to be done before we left the house as well as our first priorities for unpacking and what furniture or other items we might need for the new home.

An ultrasound is a painless procedure that uses sound waves to detect lumps or any other unusual findings. It usually takes about ten to fifteen minutes, starting with the application of cold gel to the spot where they'll do the imaging. The procedure can help determine whether an abnormality is solid, like a cancerous or benign tumor, or whether it is fluid-filled, which would be more indicative of a cyst.

As I lay there, the ultrasound tech moved the wand over the gel, taking multiple pictures along the way. Meanwhile, I stared at the pictures on the screen as the procedure progressed, hoping they would reveal something to me. Of course, they didn't. Other than what I have gleaned from the medical Internet, I have no medical training whatsoever and wouldn't even know what to look for. However, it seemed to my untrained eye that the tech took an unusual number of pictures.

Given my vast experience with medical procedures by this point, it took a lot to scare me. Nevertheless, cancer was high on the list of medical conditions that could evoke fear. I was lying there, waiting impatiently for someone to tell me there was nothing to worry about and starting to feel uncomfortable that no one was saying it.

As this was going on, one of my partners texted me from work. "Hey, sorry to bother you when you're moving, but this client needs an answer right away, and you're the only one who has worked on this."

"Well, crap," I responded. "I'm in the middle of an ultrasound right now and a conference call would be awkward, at best. Let me get back to you as soon as I'm done here."

The radiologist, Cheryl, came in after the tech finished and spent *a lot* of time with the ultrasound. She took still more pictures and appeared to be focusing on a particular spot. I had met her before and knew that she was in a book club with a friend of mine. I felt a strange kinship through that association, so we chatted. I thought I was quite clever for avoiding the elephant in the room. Instead of asking, "What the heck are you taking so many pictures of?" I asked, "So, what's the book club reading this month?"

"*The Book Thief.*"

"Do you recommend it?" I asked casually.

I get most of my reading lists from book clubs, since they've gone to all the trouble of selecting the good ones. Admittedly, this line of conversation was in part to break the awkward silence as she went back and forth, round and round, over my boobs with the ultrasound wand, stopping over what seemed to me to be the same spot over and over again to take a picture. She attempted to set my mind at ease by talking about the book, coming down on the side of recommending it.

Meanwhile, I was stressed again at the thought that I had movers at my house and had stuff to do. I also needed to figure out what to do about the client crisis that was brewing. I appreciated that Cheryl and everyone else at the Women's Center had been so nice and accommodating, but I was starting to lose my patience.

"Are we there yet?" I kept asking.

Cheryl looked up at me with an abundance of compassion and apologized that the procedure was taking so long. Finally, she looked concerned and said, "I see something that looks like a small lump, so I think we need to do a biopsy. If you want to get dressed and head back out to the front counter, they can help you schedule that."

I didn't move. I didn't get up, and I didn't get dressed, either. I thought for a nanosecond before giving Cheryl my most serious, piercing look and said, "What do I have to do to convince you to do it now? To be perfectly honest, once that moving van leaves the house, the likelihood of me coming back is, well, zero."

To my horror, they were extremely accommodating and agreed to do the biopsy on the spot. By now, I was beginning to get just a little suspicious. *This never happens*, I thought. Accommodating is one thing, but the way they made time for me had gone far beyond that.

I texted my colleague, Susan, again: "Sorry, but you've gotta tell that guy that I'm tied up for the afternoon. If it really is an emergency, get a number where he can be reached this evening, and I'll call him on my way up to the mountains."

"Why?" she asked. "What's going on?"

"Don't really know," I replied. "If I had to guess, I would say that I might have breast cancer."

I was frankly embarrassed to have said it, since I didn't want to be that woman with a headache who immediately concludes she has a brain tumor. It's just that as soon as Susan asked what was going on, that was the only response I could think of. It just slipped out.

"Noooo!" Susan texted back. "Okay, don't worry about the client. I'll see what I can do. Keep me posted on what's happening and if there's anything I can do to help."

"Will do," I said, terminating the conversation abruptly.

Once I had put it into words, for the first time I allowed myself to entertain the thought that I might, in fact, have breast cancer. Despite all the clues pointing in that direction, this was the first moment when I considered that cancer was a real possibility. Given all my distractions, though, my thought process stopped there. I didn't wonder whether surgery would be required or if I'd need chemo, radiation, or any other treatment. I didn't concern myself with the stage of the cancer, its characteristics, or even the size of the tumor. I just had one, clean thought: *I might have breast cancer.*

I may not be alone in having this type of initial reaction, since in retrospect I needed time to absorb the fundamental truth before I could stress over the details. I did, however, think this was a flashback to the idea that every positive event in my life would trigger an equal and opposite reaction. The more exciting and momentous the good—in this case, the move and the new home—the more devastating and momentous the bad—cancer, of course. *Damn it,* I thought, *let's not go down that road.*

After several minutes, Cheryl returned with an assistant. They would be doing the biopsy now, in the same room as the ultrasound, since the location of the biopsy would be guided by ultrasound. What had started as a little shove toward a blunt reality was quickly becoming a push off the cliff. My efforts at denial were becoming more difficult and therefore more creative. *Do they really need to do a biopsy just to tell me it was nothing and send me on my way?* The procedure was taking on a surreal quality. It came in stark contrast to my prior few years of medical history, consisting of concrete yet amorphous pain and other symptoms that had resulted in no definitive diagnosis.

Compared to all the medical issues I had experienced previously, this moment had seemed certain to be a nonevent. I had no pain, no lump as far as I could tell, and no other symptoms. Yet, these two medical professionals walked in the door with gravely serious facial expressions, as though I ought to be concerned. I didn't want to belittle their dramatic presentation, so I attempted to mimic their demeanor. There we were, all looking very serious as they prepared the local anesthetic and instruments for the biopsy.

The purpose of a biopsy is to remove some cells from a suspicious area and examine them under a microscope to determine a diagnosis. This involves local anesthesia, a hollow needle, and lots of poking around while extracting cell samples. Start to finish, the whole procedure takes just over an hour. The poking and prodding is all image-guided, meaning that the radiologist is looking at the ultrasound for guidance to see where they're going with that hollow needle. As one might expect, the hollow needle is large enough to leave some bruising and tenderness but no serious side effects.

For the duration of the procedure, the radiologist was entirely silent except to say, "This will pinch a little" and "Almost done." As during any medical procedure where strangers are poking and prodding areas that are not generally exposed to the public, I felt a little awkward and couldn't think of a single thing to say, witty or otherwise. I really wasn't sure how I should be feeling or reacting at this point, so I just drifted off into my own thoughts. The good and the bad were so intertwined that, in the end, I just felt numb.

Even if I have cancer, I still get to move, right? I thought. *Yikes, but what if I have to do chemo and my hair falls out? I cannot handle that. What if I die and never get to see my young adults grow into older adults? And what about radiation? Surgery? Oh crap, could this come at a worse time? Okay, take a deep breath and put all these nasty thoughts on hold. You can revisit them on the drive up to the mountains tonight . . .*

Finally, I just pointed at my face and said to Cheryl, "Look at me. I'm not crying. I'm not hysterical. So just tell me what you see."

Cheryl looked me straight in the eyes and said, "I think you have breast cancer."

That was not the answer I was looking for. As I lay there, I thought about all the Internet research I had conducted to nail down an explanation for my orthopedic problems back when I was having all the mysterious medical issues. Here I was, suddenly facing a diagnosis I didn't even think to look for. The mysterious issues I'd had eventually gave way to an illness that required no Internet research for clarification.

I felt strangely validated to have a well-defined disease that would require equally well-defined treatment. Thoughts of hair loss, surgery, and the pressing issue of my mortality haunted me. On top of that, I was flustered and embarrassed by my complete lack of knowledge as to the ways breast cancer played out. I had so many unanswered questions: *What was the next step? What types of treatment would I need? What order would they take place in? How would I feel during treatment?*

I suddenly wished I were more knowledgeable on these topics. I am certain that Cheryl didn't want to insult my intelligence by assuming that I had as little knowledge as I actually did. But I had lived the past thirty or so years in a male-dominated career, and I'd had very little girl time during which I might have learned a few things about breast cancer. Many of my neighbors and business colleagues had experienced breast cancer, but I had never delved into the details of their treatment, and they had never offered that info. I simply asked how they were doing, and most responded that they were "doing fine" without elaboration.

I found out later that, due to the location of the lump and my "dense breasts," neither I nor the standard mammography equipment could have detected the abnormality. But because I listened to my friend Jenny and got my exam using the new 3-D equipment before my move, they were able to detect it early. "Dense breasts" like mine have more "dense tissue," consisting of glandular and fibrous connective tissue, with relatively low amounts of fatty tissue. A traditional mammogram will show whether the breasts are dense or not, but certain factors associated with higher breast density, such as postmenopausal hormone replacement therapy and having a low body mass index, can muddy the results.

For women with dense breasts, a traditional mammogram can be harder to read, making it more difficult to find breast cancer. Incidentally, women with dense breasts are also at a higher risk for breast cancer in the first place. Had I waited to do my mammogram until we settled at our new home, where they did not have 3-D equipment at the time (though they do now), the cancer would not have been found in time. While I begrudged my appointment and the follow-ups, I am eternally grateful to my friend Jenny, who insisted I have the procedure done at such an inconvenient time to avail myself of the more effective technology.

My parting words to Cheryl that day were "Thank you for your candor. Can I go now? The movers, you know . . ." She could tell that she didn't have my full attention, so she let me out the door without much further discussion, except to say that my doctor would follow up with me.

I headed home in a fog. I was still uncertain if I should have a meltdown or if I should put my feelings on hold until we had confirmation from the lab. On the one hand, Cheryl seemed fairly certain of her observations when she said that she *thought* I had breast cancer. On the other hand, nothing was medically confirmed until the lab results came back. I was told that would take a couple of days and that my doctor would probably call me by Monday. I opted against the meltdown—still feeling somewhat dismissive about the informal cancer diagnosis—and refocused all my energy on moving.

In another cosmic coincidence, by the time I got home, Jenny had just stopped by the house to chat with Bob to say goodbye. As soon as I saw her, I ran over and gave her a big hug. "You should feel very good about yourself for pushing me to do the mammogram," I said and told her the news.

Jenny was stunned into silence. She told me later there was no doubt in her mind that the radiologist didn't just *think* I had cancer. Despite the gravity of the moment, I needed to help the movers with a few decisions, so Jenny and I hugged again and said our goodbyes. I promised to let her know what happened when the lab results came back.

Once I had answered the movers' questions, Bob asked how my appointment went. "It seems like you were gone for a very long time," he said.

I briefly told Bob about the ultrasound and the biopsy and mentioned to him that the radiologist thought I had breast cancer. He showed concern and wanted to talk, but we both had to move on to the task immediately at hand as the movers came bounding out the door with yet another piece of large furniture.

We drove in separate cars up to the mountains that night, so we never had a calm moment to talk about it any further that day. I don't think it really registered with Bob that I *might* have cancer, and I know it didn't really register with me that day. After all, there was no history of cancer in my family. I was obsessively fit and healthy. Cancer just wasn't my thing. So that little "you might have cancer" idea just simmered on the back burner without ever taking hold as we arrived at the new home and the movers unloaded the moving van.

When Bob and I discussed the radiologist's comment the next day, we focused heavily on the words "*I think* you have cancer" or "*you might* have cancer." Bob is literal and pragmatic. In his mind, until there is something to act on, there is no reason to worry. Unlike me, he doesn't believe in worrying over things that can't be changed, nor does he believe in speculating about something to which you can't possibly know the answer. He kept me focused on unpacking and placing the furniture and led me to compartmentalize any negative "cancer thoughts" until we had concrete information one way or the other. I was grateful for the distraction of moving, which made it easier for me to follow Bob's advice.

CHAPTER 12

THE QUEEN *of* DENIAL

MONDAY MORNING AFTER A WEEKEND of unpacking and starting to get settled into our new home, my gynecologist, Dr. Bailey, called. I was sitting in my new office, which consisted of the smallest desk possible—just big enough to hold my laptop, scanner, phone, and printer. The office, by the way, was in my bedroom. My view from this office was the forest, the golf course, and a few neighboring homes. I thought my life was looking pretty perfect, although I still had to address that nagging, but likely nothing, breast-cancer issue. As I took the call from Dr. Bailey, the physician who had ordered the mammogram, I had an uneasy feeling. When your personal physician calls you directly, you know something's not right.

Dr. Bailey was the assisting surgeon for my hysterectomy disaster, so she knows me fairly well. She started off the conversation with some small talk.

"Hey, how are you doing?" she asked.

"Oh, you know, tired. We just moved on Friday, and I'm busy unpacking."

"That must be exciting. This is the new home at Lake Tahoe?"

She was trying every trick in the book to soften the blow and to do the slow buildup, but, opting for directness, I cut her off and said, "I know. The radiologist told me."

I could tell from her tone that Dr. Bailey was not happy. Since there can't be a definitive diagnosis until the lab results are in, she reacted as though the radiologist had broken protocol. This was supposed to be *her* news to deliver, lab notes in hand. I explained to Dr. Bailey that at my insistence Cheryl had just shared what she *thought* she saw during the ultrasound. I emphasized that Cheryl had stressed "thought," and I knew that her observations were subject to confirmation by the lab. Dr. Bailey had the official news, interpreted lab results and all. For all intents and purposes, she could rest assured that she was still the official bearer of bad news.

We talked for a while about my diagnosis, and Dr. Bailey expressed shock at how often she'd been needing to make these phone calls recently. Based on my lab results, she advised that while I definitely had breast cancer, it appeared to be a less-aggressive variety. I asked what I should do next, and she advised me to contact the cancer center in San Mateo to set up an initial meeting with my treatment team, consisting of an oncologist, radiologist, and surgeon. If needed, a plastic surgeon would join the group. We also talked about the cancer statistics in various areas of California; the concept of "cancer clusters," geographic areas where higher-than-average instances of breast cancer occurs; and the fact that we had lived in Marin County—home to one of the most concentrated cancer clusters in the country. Once Dr. Bailey started throwing around terms like "cancer center" and "medical team," I finally became convinced that there was, in fact, an issue.

The conversation ran its natural course and returned back to the situation at hand, my diagnosis. Dr. Bailey shared that based on the size of the tumor—only a couple of centimeters—it could most likely be removed by a lumpectomy rather than a mastectomy. That was a source of small comfort to me. But first I would need to go to the cancer center and meet the medical team who would treat me. The San Mateo Cancer Center was in the same hospital as the Women's Center, just around the corner.

I hung up the phone and took a few deep breaths. I was well aware from yoga that this was supposed to be a calming exercise but can honestly say that under the circumstances it was not very effective. So, I called Bob from the other room and said, "That was my doctor. I do have breast cancer." Bob came into my office and asked if I was okay, and I said I was, although a couple of tears came to my eyes. We talked about the next steps, whether I would seek treatment in Tahoe or the Bay Area, and the logistics of my treatment. I assumed then that I would need to drive from the mountains to San Mateo for all my cancer treatment. Being a product of big cities, it had not even crossed my mind that there would be a decent cancer center in the small mountain town where we now lived.

As soon as I shared the news with Bob and he returned to his office in the other room, "cancer" thoughts started seeping into my mind. This time, I knew answers were out there, and I didn't want to wait to know what the details of my treatment would be. I called the San Mateo Cancer Center and begged for the earliest possible appointment, which was later that week. By the end of the day, cancer dominated my thoughts.

I immediately jumped to the conclusion that cancer would be worse than my hysterectomy experience, simply because of the anticipation of what I would be going through. Legions of hysterectomies have gone awry, but I didn't learn that until after the fact. At the time of my surgery, I'd spent zero time worrying that my hysterectomy would go south, so there had been no anxiety or apprehension about it whatsoever. As I literally signed my life away on the surgery waiver, the parade of horribles that could happen during or as a result of a hysterectomy (you could die, suffer blood clots, get infections, experience genitourinary or gastrointestinal tract injury or bleeding, or suffer nerve injury) were mere background noise. I acknowledged them as tragic things that could happen to other people but not to me. Besides, as a lawyer, I knew that the pre-op waivers were always overblown as a CYA, just in case something horrific happened. I did not suspect for a minute that anything foreshadowed by the waiver would actually happen to me.

With cancer, on the other hand, you just know going in that it's going to be a rough ride. With my new diagnosis, I spent a lot of time and effort trying to pretend that I was not freaking out inside. I mean, we all know people who have been through cancer or who didn't make it through cancer. It's in the news every day. You couldn't miss it if you tried. With all the bad press about cancer out there, the Big C scared the living crap out of me on many levels. For starters, I lived in mortal fear of losing my hair. I also viewed mastectomies as a form of mutilation. Last, but not least, is the whole mortality issue. Cancer has a bad reputation on this front. Even with forms of cancer that are curable now, it crosses your mind once in a while that things could change for the worse.

Because I feared cancer, I perpetuated my own ignorance about the details of my diagnosis and treatment. When the medical team identified my cancer as HR negative, HER2 positive, they were speaking a foreign language to me. I had no freaking clue how chemo was administered, or radiation for that matter. Needless to say, I never did the self-breast-check thing. I still don't, but post-cancer, it seems less pressing, since someone else is always on top of that for me.

Yet, much to my own surprise, and to the surprise of everyone who knew me and the emotional depths to which I am capable of sinking, I did not fall apart upon receiving the news. I was scared but resolute, more focused on finding out the details of treatment so that I could at least direct my anxiety in a specific direction.

Through diagnosis, chemo, radiation, and recovery, I shed about three tears over the whole experience, and really, they were just trickles, not heart-wrenching sob sessions. Other than the obvious lingering concerns about a recurrence—or even my mortality—my experience was, on balance, decidedly positive.

Initially, however, I relied heavily on denial to brighten my spirits. It was easy, since I had never thought I was vulnerable to cancer in the first place. Even after receiving a clear diagnosis, I didn't get the sense that this was actually happening to *me*. I don't know why exactly I thought that I had a personal exemption from cancer. Maybe my frontal lobe never fully closed, and I have the reckless confidence of a teenager. There is plenty of evidence in my life to suggest that, but I knew that if I ever did go down the cancer road, I would be an emotional basket case. Instead, denial was my go-to strategy for getting through the first few weeks, and it worked just fine.

Eventually, my denial gave way to dismay, dismay to numbness, and numbness turned to fear. Hearing the details of the treatments I would receive, the ordeal of selecting and wearing a wig, the reactions of the people I needed to tell, and the gravity of my medical team all sent me into a state of shock. Rationally, I processed the information that my type of cancer at the stage we caught it was not likely to be life-threatening. But emotionally, regardless of what you are told, mortality is one of the fear factors that you may face. I didn't plan to have a positive attitude. I fully expected an express elevator to my emotional basement. I tried to wallow but couldn't. The only option was to resolve to move forward. And that is what I did with the help of my friends, family, and medical support team.

PART FOUR:
The Coping

CHAPTER 13

FML

Laura and me, circa 1959

AFTER GETTING OFF THE PHONE with the cancer center to schedule my appointment with the medical team, I called my one and only sister, Laura. She was horrified that I had cancer and immediately asked if I had called Mom. I told her I hadn't. I needed to brace myself for that one. She asked me all kinds of questions that I didn't know the answers to and a few that I did:

"Will you have chemo? What about surgery? Are you going to get radiation? If so, when? How big is the tumor? When are you calling Mom? Do you need for me to come up there?"

I politely declined her offer to visit, given all the things I had to do and catch up on, and promised to call her as soon as I knew anything, assuring her my next call was to Mom.

She immediately texted me after we hung up: "Needless to say, you win." It might seem like an unusual reaction to the news I had just delivered, but Laura and I love gallows humor. She is the funniest and most sincere person I have ever met, and she's faced her own share of challenges in life. Sometimes, those kinds of challenges are so devastating it's not good to verbalize them. For this reason, texting has been a boon to our relationship. We can crack each other up with a few words, brighten each other's days without delving into the weeds, and move on. This is how texting "FML," and our personal FML contest, came into being. (Not to be confused with the "F My Life" contest online, which is open to the general public. Check it out at FMyLife.com)

I am committed to limiting my use of profanity in this book, trying my hardest not to offend anyone. Sometimes, though, profanity is the only thing that fits, so forgive me. "FML" is shorthand for our "f#%k my life" contest—a weekly competition won by the person who's having the suckiest life experience that week. I guess you could say it's sort of a win-lose situation. I believe a new contest starts every Monday, but we've never formalized the rules. I just know that one day, I fell flat on my face and ended up in the emergency room with a concussion and two very black eyes. I thought I was the slam dunk winner for the week, but Laura reminded me that it was only Monday, and it was way too early for her to concede. For once, nothing else bad happened that week to either of us, so I *did* get to keep the prize for the week. Laura had the privilege, though, of sharing the picture of my face with our mom, who did a primal scream and called me immediately to make sure that the possibility of brain damage had been explored and ruled out. Laura often uses my crises to deflect Mom's attention from whatever might be going on in *her* life. I am happy to grant Laura that privilege, especially if it cheers her up. Since she has always been the queen of shock value, it usually does offer her some element of delight.

As soon as she found out I had cancer, though, she created a lifetime achievement category for me in the FML contest and declared me the runaway winner. Personally, I think she has a fair claim to the top prize as well and recently challenged her on this point. While Laura couldn't deny that a fair share of crap had rained on her parade, she insisted that I keep the prize. For the time being at least, I graciously accepted. To make things official, she created an

The current version of the Lifetime Achievement Award. For now, I am the proud recipient.

actual prize: a T-shirt that Laura designed herself. In light of my challenge, she altered the design of the shirt from her first vision. It originally had the letters "FML" at the top over a trophy with the caption "Lifetime Achievement Award" to commemorate my winning. The new design shows both of us in teddies, because the only picture she could find of two women fighting over something had them both in teddies. Our faces are superimposed over the anonymous women, engaged in a tug-of-war over the trophy. Our names are listed repeatedly and crossed out when there is a new winner, which can change from week to week. In truth, sometimes declaring the winner for the week is a tough call, and I doubt we will ever agree on who the actual lifetime winner is. As a result, the prize transfers back and forth between the two of us.

The T-shirt just says "FML" for obvious reasons. If asked, I will say that it stands for "Feeling Mighty Lonely" or something like that. But you and every Millennial who reads this will know the truth. Laura would be more direct about what the initials stand for, because she is not a believer in sugar-coating anything. Were you to ever see this shirt, you may also notice that the entire shirt, including the all-important "FML" graphic, is printed backward. When I first received the shirt, I called Laura to ask her to fix it. She immediately said "FML" and hung up the phone. *Fair enough*, I thought. The very nature of the contest implies that she had more to worry about than whether or not a T-shirt was printed backward.

Please Don't Tell Me 'Bout the News

Next up, I told my mom. I had decided to just rip the proverbial Band-Aid right off, so I called her up and said bluntly, "I have breast cancer." She acted as though she hadn't heard what I said or as if she had misunderstood. When I repeated that I had just been diagnosed with breast cancer, I could tell she was trying to pretend she wasn't crying on the phone. My mom doesn't believe in lengthy phone conversations under any circumstances, but it was clear that she was in a hurry to get off the phone to process the information on her own terms that day. We just talked for a minute or two, long enough for her to ask what happens next. At that point, I still didn't know.

I was relieved to have gotten this call behind me and even more relieved that my mom managed to suck it up long enough for me to get off the phone. I'm sure that as soon as she was done crying, she called Laura. I don't know what they discussed, without any concrete information on the table as to the treatment or characterization of the cancer. Something tells me that they echoed my naïve attitude—that they certainly did not expect this from me, given my overall focus on health.

Then I called each of my daughters. They were very concerned, but getting straight to the heart of the matter, they immediately asked, "Are you gonna make it?" When I reassured them that I was, they took the news in stride and offered whatever assistance they could provide. After all, they had seen me through a much more immediate near-death experience, one that made cancer look like an abstract concept. Later, they carefully asked whether I had the BRCA gene that determines the likelihood that breast cancer is hereditary, which I confirmed I did not. I hadn't even considered that they would naturally be concerned about whether the cancer was hereditary. I am grateful I do not carry the gene so that hopefully they will be spared.

Next, I told friends, my business partners, and some of my clients. Those who, like me, only had a passing familiarity with cancer were surprised that someone who appeared as healthy as I did had cancer.

I called Jenny later in the day, and she was a great support. She cut straight to the chase and grilled me on the composition of the medical team and whatever I knew about the type and characterization of the cancer, and then she walked me through some of the events that would follow the initial meeting with the medical team. I shared everything I knew about my diagnosis and the medical team with Jenny.

"Call the cancer center back right now and schedule another appointment," was her first response. "You don't want the surgeon you were assigned to, so you need to wait until Dr. Pinelli is available."

"Are you serious?" I responded, wary of changing my appointment with the medical team. As it was, I was already on pins and needles waiting to find out the timing and nature of my treatment. She wanted me to *wait longer*?

Jenny insisted this was the right choice, assuring me that she was certain some of her friends who had experienced breast cancer would be happy to get in touch with me if I had any questions or just wanted to talk. She even offered to call them. I thanked her for the offer but didn't want to clutter my mind with other people's experiences. I would just deal with my own issues as they unfolded.

This was exactly the same way I had dealt with my pregnancies. I was aware that there were thousands of things that could go wrong, and even a routine birth could be horrifyingly painful. Every time a friend started to relay her experience, I stopped her. On the whole, I am much better at dealing with things as they present themselves, rather than working myself into a frenzy over what *could* happen.

Once again, my friend Jenny had come through for me, advising that the surgeon I had been assigned was not the superstar I'd want to have on my team. Although I was desperate to know the game plan and wanted to have the initial team meeting right away, I suppressed my natural inclination to forge ahead quickly and postponed the meeting for a week or two so I could have the surgeon Jenny thought was best. I had no idea whether waiting was the right decision. In the back of my mind, I thought a lumpectomy was child's play for surgeons anyway, so I didn't really think it mattered *who* performed the surgery. However, I trusted Jenny's judgment and worked on being more patient. It took every ounce of self-control I had and a giant leap of faith for me to call the cancer center back and reschedule the appointment, but Jenny's advice had been flawless so far, so I blindly followed this most recent recommendation as well.

After I made my announcements, I discovered that everyone I knew had a similar reaction; they all rushed to get their mammograms. Having a friend or relative diagnosed with breast cancer is the ultimate reminder that the breast defense is a good offense. By this time, I had moved over to a new law firm, where most of the partners were women. My business partners were thoughtful and supportive, offering to take any work off my hands that they could handle. One or two even cried when I shared the news with them, and all expressed their wishes that it was not aggressive and could be cured. They asked me to keep them in the loop on my schedule for surgery and treatment so they could be prepared to cover for me if necessary. They also sent me beautiful flowers. I placed the flowers on the kitchen island, where they would be visible from most of the downstairs area of our home. They were a constant reminder that there was another world outside of cancer and that there were people out there who cared about what I was going through.

For a lot of reasons, I was reluctant to pass on much of my work. I was anxious to convince my clients that their work would be handled seamlessly, regardless of how I was feeling. I didn't share my diagnosis with all my clients, only those with whom I had worked long enough that we also had a personal relationship. Some clients never knew that I had cancer at all. In any case, I was the only attorney at my firm that specialized in the niche I had chosen, except for Susan, the colleague I had exchanged texts with from the Women's Center. She was still in the training process, however, so if I had checked out for a few weeks, much of the business I had built over the course of my entire real estate career could have been lost to competitors.

For the most part, I had to just steel through it and hope that I would be in a condition to handle any client crises as they occurred. Under the best of circumstances, there were often situations where I could not respond immediately to a client's concerns: real meetings, family or personal obligations (a.k.a. fake meetings), business travel, site tours, seminars, and speaking engagements, to name a few. These were the excuses I used in my out-of-office messages when I went to chemo sessions or simply needed a nap.

As I finished the obligatory phone calls, I was relieved to be able to check this task off my list and refocus on the other things that I needed to do. Sharing personal news was never my forte, so this task had weighed heavily on my mind. The next things on my list involved preparing for the unknown. I didn't know when I would have surgery, how I would feel afterward, whether or not I would have chemo and radiation, and what the effects would be if I did. So, I got busy unpacking and catching up on work so I could disappear for a few days, if necessary, without causing my clients any panic. I also wanted the house to be reasonably comfortable and organized so that I wouldn't have to be constantly searching for things, just in case I would not feel up to it when everything started to hit the fan.

CHAPTER 14

HAIR TODAY, *Gone* TOMORROW

REMEMBER THE LYRICS FROM THE musical *Hair*? All my life, I had pursued that long, beautiful hair. I think I had long hair for so many years due to the emotional scars I had suffered from the pixie cut I wore as a child, though its beauty was often questionable.

My generation was just a teeny step behind the Summer of Love. In 1968, I was twelve. When Janis Joplin was at her peak, my best friend and I did a tag team imitation of Janis: She did the voice, and I was the hair. Left to its natural state, my hair is curly, frizzy, and uncontrollable—the bane of my existence! After all, in that era we all wanted to look like the actress Peggy Lipton, with stick-straight hair. Living in San Francisco, I blow-dried, flat-ironed, hair-sprayed, and conditioned the unruly mop for hours on end, only to walk out in the fog, which made all my efforts go up in smoke.

Finally, in my fifties, I discovered keratin treatments, also referred to as a "Brazilian blowout." I came to love my hair for the first time in my life. The treatments left it straight and healthy for six full months. I finally felt victorious over the lifelong love/hate relationship I'd had with my hair. In short, I was my own Pantene poster child.

Given my decades of hair struggles, I will admit, sheepishly, that on occasion, when hearing about another woman's ordeal with cancer, I actually thought the worst part of the illness was losing your hair. I lived in mortal fear of chemo, for all the wrong reasons. This was phenomenally vain and shallow, I know, but I can't deny having the thought. In a pathetic attempt at self-forgiveness, I like to think that I am not the first or only person to have had this thought. Two of my friends recently validated my line of thinking when we were out walking our dogs. They admitted that the potential for losing their hair had always been in the forefront of their thoughts about cancer. They reminded me that after World War II, shaving the heads of French women who were seen as Nazi collaborators and parading them through the public streets was considered the ultimate act of censure for a woman. And in *Game of Thrones*, the same theme is repeated when Queen Cersei's head is shaved and she is required to do a "walk of shame" before the entire city. So, maybe my concerns about losing my hair weren't so shallow or unique after all.

I'm going to address the hair issue right up front, because it was so central to my fear of cancer. When I had my initial meeting with my oncology team, they disseminated lots of information, including handfuls of brochures with helpful information that I never read. What I remember from this meeting could be distilled into one sentence: "Fourteen days after you start chemo, your hair will fall out." Although part of me was mortified by that prediction, I was startled to find that the scientific precision of the statement was intriguing. Let me say, it did not disappoint. Fourteen days after the first treatment, I was combing conditioner through my hair when suddenly most of it fell to the bench in my shower.

The only portion of the informational materials provided by the medical team that I did read was the referrals to wig salons, which was new territory for me. Before all my hair fell out, I wanted to be prepared. So, I chose to go to Wig 'N Out, mostly because the name resonated with me but also because a nurse owned the store. I'm not sure why that mattered, except that nurses have seen it all, and I had had such positive experiences with nurses that I felt as if she would have a better understanding of my state of mind than a lay person. As it turned out, she was compassionate and caring and didn't fuss a lot about cancer, just on the selection of a wig. My husband and I stopped at her shop on our way out of town for the weekend. We were meeting friends in forty-five minutes to drive up to their cabin on Huntington Lake, so we'd been on a very tight schedule that day.

"Jen"

When we walked into the wig salon, I noticed dozens of styles to choose from, but most were just not my taste. Because matronly was not on my list of desired looks, many choices fell rapidly by the wayside, much like my real hair would in the shower a few weeks later. After walking around the store, I decided that I just wanted to replicate my current keratin-treated look as much as possible. Along came "Jen," my favorite wig, which I named after the actress Jennifer Aniston, as she and the wig sported the same hairstyle.

I'd have to say that the first shocker in my whole cancer experience, other than the thought of losing all my hair, was that my

"Farrah"

insurance covered the cost of wigs! The owner of Wig 'N Out clued me in on this, so I called my insurance company right from the shop. Sure enough, they were going to spring for the wigs, to the tune of $700 bucks. *Woohoo, we're shopping now!* I thought, deciding that I might actually need *two* wigs, since Jen only cost about half of what the insurance would pay.

I decided to go with synthetic hair wigs rather than real hair, since I found the fake ones looked just fine once I found a style that I could live with. In a major 1970s flashback, the next wig I chose was "Farrah." Any good Boomer remembers the Revlon commercials with Farrah Fawcett's beautiful, long shag 'do. I decided that Farrah would be my party wig, and Jen would be my everyday wig.

After wig shopping that afternoon, Bob and I headed up to Huntington Lake. Two other couples were there for the weekend. As we sat on the deck overlooking the lake, enjoying our eggs and bacon the next morning, one of the women revealed that she dyed her own hair. Up until then, I never had considered the do-it-yourself option. I've always had blond hair with highlights, which are too challenging to do yourself. But then, I thought, *What the heck, I've got nothing to lose. In less than a month, I won't have any hair.* I decided right then that I would dye my own hair before it fell out, just to experiment with a color I wouldn't otherwise have had the nerve to try.

I perused the various shades of auburn on the shelf at Rite Aid when we got home and chose "Power Red." It wasn't really me, but at least I had gotten that out of my system. And when my auburn hair fell out in the shower a few weeks later, I realized I had unwittingly taken my denial one step further, since it didn't even look like my hair.

But I was ready. I was beginning to realize that Jen and Farrah might make me look better than I did without a wig, so with Jen and Farrah by my side, I could handle anything.

The Higher the Pedestal, the Harder the Fall

As can be expected, the insurance industry was only on a pedestal for a fleeting moment. Just days later, they actually had the *cojones* to deny payment for the 3-D mammogram, because there was no medical proof that it was any better than cheaper methods for detecting cancer. I tried to process the logic: *The methodology that detected my cancer and, by the way, is the only methodology that would have detected it is no good at detecting cancer? Really?*

The litigator in me sprang into action, and I was ready to wage WWIII against my insurance company and expose its messed-up, self-serving logic to the world. I couldn't let go of my shock that they would spring for two wigs but not the mammogram with state-of-the-art equipment. In my mind, this was a graphic demonstration of how insurance companies have made themselves easy targets for criticism (and lawsuits).

I'm certain we could collectively rail on insurance companies with thousands of examples of how they've gotten carried away with their power, but it's probably best not to dwell on this for too long—unless it's your only option for obtaining treatment. Unfortunately, I am intimately familiar with some of their bad behavior, having represented insurance companies during my early years as an attorney. My goal, in this instance, was to make this insurance company sorry it ever existed. Just as I was determining my strategy and marshaling my resources for the onslaught on the company, the Women's Center volunteered to absorb the charge for the mammogram right out of the box, taking the angry wind right out of my sails. I resented that money from the Women's Center was spent on something that should have been insured, certain that there were better uses for it. But the fact that they so readily accepted accountability for the charge made me feel as if I would be well taken care of, regardless of the cost. Although I was disappointed not to be able to take my anger out on the company that deserved it, I came to the conclusion that I didn't have to wage the war against the insurance company and that my energy was better spent on other things.

The day I went wig shopping, I remembered that my Bay Area oncologist, Josh, had told me some of the women he treated actually had some fun with the wigs. This caused me a momentary lack of confidence in his judgment, to say the least. I soon discovered there was some truth to what he said. By the time you start wearing a wig, you have already had a few weeks to let the concept sink in. I found myself no longer fighting whether or not I would wear a wig. Instead, I was just figuring out the logistics of what that entailed. Before I purchased the wigs, I knew that wigs could be uncomfortable, hot, and annoying. But there were several benefits to wearing a wig that I didn't appreciate before I wore one routinely. Wigs are costumes. When you put one on, you can play dress up just like when you were five and dressing up for Halloween. With a wig, you can be ready to go out, perfectly coiffed, at a moment's notice. Nothing messes with a wig, not even fog.

I did enjoy the fact that I could change my look from Jen to Farrah and back again as easily as I could change my clothes. Many of my male professional contacts complimented me on my hair during this period, saying it looked better than ever! All those keratin treatments, hours with the blow dryer, haircuts and coloring, and even hair washing were cut out for now. I washed the wigs about once a month and left them on the stand to dry. Most of the time, I didn't even need to brush them. It was liberating. If we're being perfectly honest, I did not see that coming.

At this point, I became aware of another tremendous benefit from the move to our new home, again in the vanity department. In our new location, I was anonymous. I could go to restaurants, Safeway, CVS, the post office, the bank, or wherever and not run into anyone I knew. I had also moved to a location where wearing a baseball cap constituted dressing up. So, I could have gone without the wig except for work. I can't begin to express how happy this made me. I could put on any funky scarf or hat and go out in public, and no one would raise an eyebrow. I never had to endure all the well-wishers gawking and saying, "Oh my God, I had no idea! I'm so sorry." When it comes from a close friend, that's one thing, but coming from a mom from the softball team that your kid was on in the eighth grade whose name you no longer remember, it seems overly personal, intrusive even. I relished the fact that I could forgo that experience.

The only grocery store encounter I did have during my cancer treatment still makes me smile. I was wearing one of my funky scarf or hat things at Safeway and was approached by a woman I had never met.

"Oh, God, I've been there," she said compassionately. "I hope you're going to 'the cancer spa,'" she added tentatively. I burst out laughing, because that was *precisely* how I referred to the local cancer center in my own mind.

Looking back on this whole hair experience, I recall one friend's comment when I told her what I was going through. Bear in mind that this is the friend with the perennially perfect hair.

"You don't define yourself by your hair; you'll be fine," she said dismissively.

She was right, though. My hair had always been the bane of my existence, not my defining quality. Her offhand comment stuck with me through chemo and gave me a surprising perspective on the importance of hair in my life, which I carry with me to this day. I now appreciate every day that my hair looks even marginally presentable. My hairstylist has convinced me to grow it long, which I have not resisted, because I still haven't gotten over that "the more the better" concept that my cancer treatment left behind.

PART FIVE:

The Treatment

CHAPTER 15

THERE'S NO "I" *in* TEAM

HAVING ADDRESSED MY HAIR TRAUMA up front, I feel as if I can now share what my first meeting with my doctors was like in the wake of my diagnosis. My oncologist, radiologist, surgeon, and I met to decide on a course of treatment, or—more accurately—so I could learn the course of treatment dictated by the characteristics of my cancer.

When the meeting finally occurred, I was impressed. It was the only time in my extensive medical experience that all the treating physicians for my condition were in one room. It signaled to me right off the bat that cancer would be different. This was a more precise science. The treatment would be coordinated among the various specialists. Everyone knew what to do, and there was a clear game plan. The biopsy, ultrasound, and mammogram had told the team a lot about what they were dealing with, and from there the entire treatment protocol took over. Each physician discussed their area of expertise and how it fit into my overall treatment. They pointed out the risks, enumerated the decision points along the way that could change the course of treatment, and discussed what

I could expect moving forward. Then they let me ask questions. I'm sure I had a few, like "How soon will the surgery be? When will you know if I need chemo? What determines that? How certain are you that my hair will fall out fourteen days after I start chemo?"

The biggest uncertainty, they shared with me, was whether or not I would have chemo, which would be decided after the lumpectomy. Since the purpose of chemo is to kill the cancer cells, one of the factors in that decision would be whether the cancer had spread and, if so, how much. That information would be revealed from the lab work following the lumpectomy. I was told that, depending upon the findings from the surgery, a mastectomy was also still a possibility, although not likely, given the size of the tumor.

We already knew, however, that the characterization of my cancer was HR positive, HER2 negative. HER refers to the human epidermal growth factor, a protein that occurs on the surface of breast-cancer cells. HER2 positive means the cancer is more aggressive. So, if I had actually paid attention to what everyone was saying, the good news was that my HER2-negative cancer was not aggressive. HR positive means the cancer cells grow in response to estrogen and/or progesterone. This is where the risk of hormone replacement therapy after menopause comes into play. The estrogen therapy that is often prescribed can fuel the growth of cancerous cells, and in my case, it apparently did. That was all great information, but I never processed it during the course of my treatment, much less during the preliminary meeting. All that I digested that day, besides the chemo-related hair loss information, was that I would first have a lumpectomy, to find the margins of the tumor and discover whether it had spread to my lymph nodes. After the lumpectomy there was the possibility of chemo, then radiation.

Chapter 16

KEEPING *the* SISTERS

I ONCE HEARD A MALE friend ask a woman going through breast cancer if she had gotten to keep the sisters. It took me longer than it should have to realize that he was asking if she'd had a mastectomy. Even more time elapsed before I thought, *What the hell? Is that the first thing that comes into his mind? Could this guy be more of an insensitive jerk?* In my mind this was an example of the wrong thing to say as a conversation opener with a cancer patient. Maybe you could work it in later in the conversation after something like "Are you okay? Can we drop off dinner tomorrow night? We're here if you need anything." Even then, I would recommend proceeding with caution.

Although my treatment outline was grim, overall the news that I would most likely need a lumpectomy and not a mastectomy was huge in my mind. The role of breasts in our society is often ridiculous (hence, the silly lawyer joke that I shared earlier), but nevertheless, the prospect of a mastectomy was chilling. Since breasts have never been my most dominant feature, and I'm one hundred percent comfortable with that, I had never focused much on how they were perceived, except to know that there are people out there who lose their senses over them.

But now I was thinking of life with or without breasts and comforted myself by focusing on the silliest manifestations possible. I mean, there is a chain of restaurants named after these body parts, for gawd sakes! The primary job qualification for waitresses is a set of giant gazongas. Of course, the uniform consists of tight T-shirts to display them. And check out the uniforms for the Dallas Cowboys' cheerleaders. It's clear what they are promoting. Then there's all the nomenclature. People who behave badly or stupidly are called "boobs." Janet Jackson's "nip slip" is still remembered several years after the fact. How many women have had a conversation where a man stared at their breasts instead of looking them in the eyes? (Just for fun, Google "My Eyes Are Up Here"). Women undergo elective surgery for breast implants that may even put their lives at risk, given the potential impact on their immune system and the risk of leaks. After all of that, I'm not entirely sure that these risks and sacrifices are fully appreciated by their intended audience.

I could go on. Suffice it to say there is enormous and undue emphasis on a body part that people can happily live without. I have the pleasure of knowing a number of women who have done preemptive strikes by undergoing radical bilateral mastectomies at the first sign or threat of cancer or even because they carry the BRCA gene. Their lives have not suffered from that decision. Quite the contrary: I believe the decision gave them peace of mind and spared them a lot of cancer treatment.

I also learned at the medical team meeting that even if I did need a mastectomy, reconstruction could now be done during the same surgery or shortly thereafter. This was news to me. I understood that it was recommended because stretching the skin out later was more challenging than doing implants before any scarring occurred.

Maybe I didn't even need to think about life without breasts, since skipping that step was now an option. When I heard this news, it was a tremendous relief, since my thinking had not yet fully evolved to the understanding that breasts were just another non-essential body part. In the blur of the initial outline of treatment, it was reassuring to know that I could have perky new ones right off the bat as a consolation prize for my cancer experience. Again, from a cosmetic perspective, this meant a lot.

CHAPTER 17

TAKING *Your* LUMPS

SINCE I WAS NOW LIVING four hours away from the Bay Area, after the team meeting, I had to decide whether to have treatment in San Mateo, where I knew several members of the medical community that would be treating me, or in the mountains, where I had no information about the facilities, equipment, or doctors. Because the surgeon, Dr. Pinelli, wanted to go forward with the lumpectomy soon, I decided to complete that part of the process in my old neighborhood and make a decision for the rest of the treatment afterward.

As a patient who was no stranger to surgery, from my perspective, the lumpectomy itself was no big deal. The idea was to remove the tumor and one lymph node, then test that lymph node to see whether the cancer had spread to other locations. In my case, my surgeon made two separate incisions, one at the lumpectomy site and another to remove the lymph node. The science behind this is really cool and was new to me at the time: Dye is injected into the lymph nodes to see which one carries the dye to other parts of the body the fastest. The lymph node winning that race is known as the sentinel node and is removed for testing. If the sentinel node is cancerous, it is likely that the cancer has spread. In my case, the lymph node showed just a few traces of cancerous cells, but those traces were what led my oncologist to conclude that chemo was the best option. While I was panicked about losing my hair, I knew the oncologist well enough to respect his opinion. I knew now that I had to deal with my fears about chemo, but I still had a few weeks to adjust before I really had to face the reality of it.

My lumpectomy was done under general anesthesia, with which I am quite familiar, and the recovery was pretty swift and painless. However, nobody had mentioned the dreaded "Dixie cup" at my team meeting (or if they had, I wasn't paying attention). Before the surgery, an ultrasound is required to isolate the exact location of the tumor for the surgeon. Once the ultrasound was done, from what I could tell, it seemed as if nails were driven into my chest so the surgeon would know where to dig. I'm certain in retrospect that they were not actually nails, but they felt that way at the time. A Dixie cup was put on over the nails to prevent them from moving. Then, since the radiology department was nowhere near the operating room, I was wheeled through what seemed like the entire hospital—Dixie cup, nails, and all. I looked down as I was steered through the halls, hoping not to see anyone I knew in this close-knit community. My gown covered the small structure, but you could still tell that there was something that looked strangely like a Dixie cup underneath. Every movement of my gown resulted in an excruciating readjustment of the nails. So, it's best not to move, should you find yourself in this situation.

Once the lumpectomy was done, the tissue removed from the breast was sent to the pathology lab, where it was tested to identify the type of tumor, determine whether lymph nodes were involved, and assess the tumor for hormone sensitivity (i.e., estrogen and progesterone receptors). Other testing may be done to help determine the prognosis and best course of treatment. My oncologist also ordered oncotyping, a genomic test analyzing the activity of a group of twenty-one genes from a breast-cancer tissue sample. The information obtained through this test helps determine how a cancer is likely to behave and respond to treatment. The test results assign a recurrence score—a number between zero and one hundred—reflecting the risk that your cancer will recur. In my case, my early-stage, estrogen-receptor-positive breast cancer was likely to recur, so my surgeon warned me that he would be likely to recommend chemotherapy once we had all the information back from the testing done during the lumpectomy.

Usually it takes several days after the lumpectomy to identify the type of tumor and to receive the other test results. Waiting for anything has always been torture for me, and this was no exception. I imagined all the worst possible results: that the cancer had spread, that I would have to go through chemo, that I would have the hereditary gene, and that the cancer was more aggressive than had originally been thought. As usual, Bob had a much more logical philosophy and tried to convince me not to worry about things that were still unknown or that I couldn't change. I understood he was making perfect sense, but I was still unable to limit my worrying to the things we already knew.

That was when I started to think about shopping for Jen and Farrah.

CHAPTER 18

MARGIN *of* ERROR

BECAUSE DR. PINELLI WAS ON vacation, I had a post-surgery follow-up appointment with the surgeon to whom I had initially been assigned. The stand-in physician showed me the surgical report and assured me that the margins were clear, meaning that they could not see any cancer cells at the margins of the tissue removed during the lumpectomy. At a rapid clip, which to the uninitiated sounded very efficient, she pointed out several phrases in the report that proved her point. By the time of the appointment, I also had what I thought was a raging infection at the surgical site where they had removed the lymph node. The site was painful and so swollen that I referred to it as my third boob. The physician assured me that I was overreacting, stating there was no infection and that this was a normal result of the surgery. I left the office feeling like a whiner for having assumed that I had an infection just because the area around my scar was puffy and yellow.

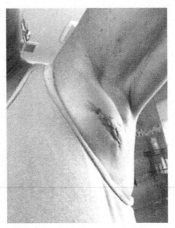

Really? Does this even look normal to a lay person?

At another routine follow-up appointment a week or two later, I met with Dr. Pinelli, the doctor who had performed the surgery, now back from vacation.

She entered the room with some trepidation and asked, "What did the other doctor tell you?"

I promptly responded, "That the margins were clear, there was no infection, and I was good to go. Why?"

When Dr. Pinelli saw the site of the incision to remove the lymph node, her facial expression became grim.

"You absolutely have an infection," she said. "We need to drain this." I was feeling grateful for having my concerns about an infection validated, until she added, "Oh, by the way, the margins were not clear. The other doctor misread the report."

I thought I had been a good sport for the first surgery, but I hadn't considered the possibility of a second one, especially after the flagrantly inaccurate report from the first surgeon. Dr. Pinelli shared that if the margins weren't clear after the second surgery, a mastectomy would be required. This new, albeit accurate, information was starting to dampen my spirits.

Dr. Pinelli walked me through all the indicators that the margins were not clear from the same report that the previous physician had glossed over in her pseudo-efficient manner. At this point, I was somewhat mortified that the surgeon I almost went to could not correctly read a pathology report and didn't know an infection when it was staring her in the face. My good friend Jenny was the best for suggesting I go with Dr. Pinelli. A couple of years later, I checked the roster at my surgeon's office and was pleased to see that the one who had misread the report was no longer there.

A week or two after meeting with Dr. Pinelli, I had another lumpectomy. This time the margins were, in fact, clear, and I had no resulting infection. There was no Dixie cup either, since there was a fresh scar to mark the spot. I was, however, left with about a two-inch scar and a dent in my left breast where my lumpectomies were done. For some reason, I had always thought that fat would fill in the space where the lump was removed. But it remains a dent. I have another scar where the lymph node was removed. None of this is noticeable either through a bathing suit or regular clothes. To me, it's visible through a sports bra, but I doubt that too many of my workout buddies are staring long enough to figure out what it is.

Decisions, Decisions . . .

Since the sentinel lymph node showed just a few cancer cells, I was on the borderline of current medical opinion as to whether or not chemo was appropriate, so my medical team left it up to me to make the decision. Because chemo was such an emotionally charged decision, I punted to my oncologist Josh and asked him point blank, "If this were your wife, what would you recommend?"

He responded without hesitation that he would recommend chemo, so that's what we decided.

While I wasn't thrilled at having chemo, Josh was actually a friend for whom I had the utmost respect. His wife, Ellen, had managed our daughter's soccer team for many years, and our families had spent lots of time on the road at soccer tournaments together. We'd endured and survived the ups and downs of team emotions and parental politics that go with children's sports teams. Josh had an air of confidence as a doctor, which I needed and respected. Over the years, I had also learned through the grapevine of his excellent reputation as an oncologist, which is why when I initially learned that the cancer center had assigned him to my medical team, I breathed a sigh of relief. One of my law partners had been his roommate in undergraduate school, so I had even more of an inside track on his reputation. Given our history and all the information about his stellar reputation that I had gathered along the way, his opinions carried a lot of weight.

Coincidentally, Ellen had also been my anesthesiologist for a couple of my orthopedic issues. I have a clear memory of the bunion surgery where she was on duty. It was a couple of years after the soccer era came to a close for us, and we had lost touch. The surgery was at our local hospital, and I requested Ellen because she was so highly regarded. For my bunion surgery, general anesthesia was only part of the process. After ten minutes or so, I awakened, and just my foot was frozen for the remainder of the surgery. Ellen and I started to chat. We might as well have been at Starbucks sharing a latte. We talked incessantly for the remainder of the surgery. We caught up on the soccer team members, shared stories about what our kids were up to, and laughed a lot. The surgeon remarked that he had never seen anyone talk so much during surgery.

An unforeseen consequence was that the surgeon felt left out. He tried to get our attention and join in the conversation a few times, but we ignored him for the most part. I assumed he was busy anyway and didn't think it was appropriate to include him in our chatter. Finally, he held my foot up to show me the stitches he had just put in place, looking for admiration of his handiwork. Ellen and I praised the foot and his lovely needlework and, hopefully, made it back into his good graces.

Now that I knew I would be having chemo, I tried to readjust my expectations and plan for the next few months, when I didn't know if I would be out of circulation. To prepare for the unknown, I readjusted my work assignments and took care of some clients' needs far in advance of their expectations so that they wouldn't need me for a while. I also finished unpacking at a furious rate. I wanted my home to feel settled and comfortable before starting chemo so I wouldn't come home to a mess and feel obligated to do all of that work if I really wasn't up to it.

I made two decisions that were atypical for me. Since I trusted Josh's opinions so much, I decided not to do any Internet research (for once in my life), since it would only raise questions based on patients whose situation may have varied from mine in critical ways I would not understand. I preferred not to clutter my mind with details that were not vital to my next steps. Besides, most of my prior Internet medical research was done in an effort to identify a condition, and I really didn't see any benefit to researching some-thing when I knew what it was. It may have been helpful to get more information about the process of chemo, but the cancer cen-ter had provided me with a small loose-leaf binder to provide a basic preview of all the aspects of treatment, if I chose to read it in any detail. I skimmed it, and that was enough for me. I didn't want to know more than that.

For those of you with a friend or relative going through chemo who does want company during the treatment, I offer you my thoughts on that role. Be forewarned that there is an awkward moment that comes with chemo hand-holding: "What are we going to talk about?" Cancer may be too depressing, but that shouldn't stop you from asking how they are feeling. Ignoring what is happening and engaging entirely in small talk may be too superficial. Bringing magazines or a favorite book to a chemo treatment may be just the thing. If your friend is technologically competent, audio books are the best. With a set of headphones, they can relax and close their eyes and still be reading a book. Chemo treatments can be a mini book club. Read the same book, then find some book club questions online. Bring a deck of cards, just in case. If there is a deafening silence, this is where the books and magazines come in handy. Even if the patient is not interested in reading, you can pretend to peruse them and come up with meaty topics for discussion if an awkward silence needs to be broken. Consider that maybe the patient doesn't feel like talking. Bring something to keep yourself engaged, and just talk if they want to. That way, they also choose the topic and relieve you of that burden.

My second unusual decision was that I didn't want anyone to go with me for any of the chemo sessions. I would work, read a book, or nap during my sessions, but I didn't want to chat or, even worse, have someone stare at me, waiting for some kind of reaction. I allowed Bob to drop me off and pick me up for the first session, since I didn't know how I would feel, but that was it. I think a large part of this decision came from the fact that I didn't have a clue what I would say to someone undergoing chemo, so I didn't have the confidence that anyone else would know what to say to me either. I think I underestimated everyone else, but I was very content with my decision to go it alone. Left to my own devices, I can easily direct my thoughts to work or a good book, but when faced with another person, I feel obliged to either talk with them or sit in awkward silence. So, I voted for my self-distraction techniques, which are more reliable and comfortable for me.

$\mathcal{T}\!he$ CANCER SPA

AFTER THE SECOND LUMPECTOMY, I still had to decide where to go for the remainder of my treatment. As you may have guessed, knowing who was who in the medical community had already become an important factor in my cancer treatment, but the chemo center in San Mateo was located in a building across the parking lot from a Safeway. I'd heard rumors that people clambered for the closely-spaced chemo chairs by the windows. Plus, there was no privacy. I didn't find this very tempting. In fact, this information was enough to push me to consider other options.

During the first week after our arrival in Truckee, a small town just northwest of Lake Tahoe, Bob and I toured the cancer facility that was five or six miles from our new home. The center was just a couple of years old and was anything but ordinary. It had received funding from Gene Upshaw, an NFL player for the Oakland Raiders, a pro football Hall of Fame inductee and a Tahoe resident. Gene Upshaw was the first player in NFL history to reach the Super Bowl in three different decades with the same team. Following a sixteen-year career in the NFL, he worked for the rights of pro football players as a player representative, officer, and ultimately as chairman of the National Football League Players Association. In mid-August 2008, his breathing became labored, resulting in a visit to the ER, where he was diagnosed with pancreatic cancer. He died three days later.

His family established the Gene Upshaw Memorial Fund. In partnership with the Tahoe Forest Health System, the Gene Upshaw Memorial Tahoe Forest Cancer Center came into being. The golf course at our new community hosts the annual Gene Upshaw Memorial Golf Classic. Gene Upshaw and his wife, Terri, were local celebrities. Gene's story and reputation as an accomplished athlete, a leader in his community, and a leader in the NFL sparked my interest.

On its website, the stated mission of the Gene Upshaw Cancer Center is "to provide the most current and appropriate high-quality cancer care with honesty, support, and compassion." Without having toured or been treated in any other cancer center, I believe they have met their goal. The setting and design are comfortable and calming. As you walk in the main entrance, there is a cozy, open seating area. Adjacent is a small room with a latte machine, snacks, and a wealth of cancer literature, along with wigs, hats, and scarves donated by the community and the American Cancer Society. To the far side of that area is the massage room. The two massage therapists are specifically trained in treating cancer patients. Patients are offered one free massage per week during cancer treatment. The free massage option definitely captured my interest, since I have always been a big fan of massage therapy. I hadn't realized there would be benefits offered to cancer patients beyond the necessary medical treatment.

Upon arrival, I was immediately greeted by the receptionists, and after putting on the wrist band and checking to make sure I hadn't forgotten my birth date, we chatted. One of the receptionists was pregnant, so we talked about that for a while. The baby, a boy, was her first, and she was feeling great. She may have asked how I was doing in general but never expressed pity for me or my condition. Instead, we talked about my recent move to Truckee, how long she had lived there, and other mundane, non-cancer topics. Talking about her baby and Truckee was far more uplifting than any cancer conversation could have been. Also, since pretty much everyone who walks in the door of the cancer center has cancer, pity feels out of place. For me, especially, I liked that I was being treated like a *normal* person and not a *sick* person. I found this personal yet professional approach to be the standard at this cancer center, and I appreciated the consideration given to the feelings of the patients, which had clearly gone into the decision to establish this approach.

One day, when I noticed that the receptionist had received some flowers, I admired them, and she started to cry a little bit. Her father had just died of cancer the day before. She had never mentioned that he was sick and would not have shared this had I not commented about the flowers. But, after a few sessions, we were starting to feel like a family, so I pried a little—as any family member would.

Checking in for my first appointment was very much like checking in for a spa treatment. The receptionists offered to make me a latte. After that, they signed me up for a massage and for acupuncture treatments. They also handed me materials describing onsite counseling, exercise programs designed for cancer patients, and some other offerings at the center. They even signed me up for a two-hour makeup session, which brought home the spa connection for me.

The makeup session was offered through the American Cancer Society. It was referred to as "Look Good, Feel Better." Even if you think the name sounds a little trite, when facing cancer, there's a lot of logic to it. If your mirror shows a pathetic-looking face, no eye-brows or eyelashes, wig askew or a head covered with a poorly tied scarf, you will feel like a pathetic sick person. However, if you can fool yourself into thinking that you look normal, you will *feel* more normal, which helped me immensely. Strangely, I kept my eye-brows and eyelashes through chemo and radiation, only to watch them fall out abruptly at the end of my treatment. I realized that they've never quite grown back when I was chatting with a friend about whether I should get eyelash extensions. "I think you have to have something to attach them to" was her response.

Lunch for the makeup session was catered, and the major makeup companies like Estée Lauder donated free makeup to complement the patient's coloring. There were two cosmetologists and only two patients in attendance at the session. All in all, I was impressed. I was thrilled to have two hundred dollars' worth of free makeup and all the free beauty advice I could soak up over the course of the two-hour session. Unlike my daughters, who can apply flawless eyeliner in a moving car, my makeup skills have always been limited. The other patient and I grilled the cos-metologists for all the makeup advice we could think of. In addi-tion to the general advice on cosmetics, they demonstrated some cancer-specific tips, including how to draw eyebrows when you have none as a frame of reference, and what colors to use if you're lacking your usual glow. We also learned how to emphasize our good features for when chemo makes you look like crap, in addi-tion to how to put on a wig and one thousand and one ways to tie a scarf. I was a novice at this, only about two weeks into wearing a wig, and learned some handy little tips, like pulling on the front of the wig, then adjusting it over the back. The cosmetologists asked for a volunteer to demonstrate the scarf-tying options, but I was too self-conscious at that stage to take off my wig in front of strangers, so after a brief standoff, the other woman volunteered.

I also took advantage of the latte machine at the cancer center on every visit and still look forward to my lattes at follow-up appointments. Over the course of my treatment, I had more than my share of the free snacks, one or two free massages per week, and acupuncture—which can help minimize nausea and other side effects. The center also offered cooking and nutrition classes for patients and their caregivers, and even one massage per week for caregivers. Since Bob's motto with regard to strangers is "Don't touch my skin," he did not take them up on the massage offer. Nevertheless, it was nice that they offered to treat those caregivers who were open to receiving the treatments. An illness or other trauma can be taxing on the caregiver, friends, and relatives of the patient too, so it makes sense that they'd get some of the perks as well.

There were yoga classes designed for cancer patients, and the cancer center offered transportation to and from appointments, grocery shopping assistance, meal delivery, support groups, and counseling. The chemo room was spacious, including a beautiful fireplace feature in the middle and cozy alcoves for each patient— in my case not only providing privacy but also allowing me to get a lot of work done during chemo sessions. When checking in for chemo, gourmet selections were offered for lunch. "Will you be having the steak with Béarnaise sauce today or would you prefer the fillet of sole?" I'm sure by now you are gathering how it can be easy to confuse a chemo day at the center with an actual spa day.

By the end of my treatment, I considered the staff, doctors, nurses, technicians, and receptionists to be my friends and family, which was relatively easy, since I didn't have friends or family in the area yet. For the first few months after my arrival in Tahoe, I spent more time at the cancer center than anywhere else outside of my home. And when I return for follow-up appointments now, I look forward to reconnecting with them. A very telling fact is that most of the staff that I knew three years ago during my treatment are still there. The vibe is good, and the people are understanding, not obsequious or patronizing. The staff seem to enjoy their work, despite the recurring cancer theme.

The spa-like environment clearly tipped the scales in favor of local treatment, but there were other factors that drove my decision to go there. One piece of information disseminated at the first team meeting was that everyone responds differently to the same combo of drugs, and there is no way to predict how you will respond. There is no correlation between your physical condition prior to chemo and your tolerance for the drugs-slash-poison. I was told "You may be able to work, you may be completely flattened, or anywhere in between." Until you're in the midst of it, you just don't know. I had no idea whether I would be able to drive after chemo, or even function on any level. For these reasons, local treatment began to have a lot of appeal.

Having radiation far from home was also a challenge. In my case, radiation was to be done daily, five days a week, for six consecutive weeks. Since we had already leased our home in the Bay Area, I would need to arrange for accommodations during this time if I opted for treatment there. The cost of staying in a hotel for six weeks was a nonstarter, nor did I wish to impose on any of our friends for that amount of time. Staying with friends might also have involved socializing, and I didn't know if I would be up to that. It was only later in the process—because I had tossed out the brochures they gave me—that I found out that my situation was not unique and that the American Cancer Society partners with hotels for just this purpose. So, should you or a loved one find yourselves in a similar predicament, know that there are a number of hotels that provide deep discounts for people undergoing radiation treatment.

All things considered, I was coming to the realization that the trek to San Francisco for treatment might be an added burden that

I didn't want to deal with. I called my oncologist Josh again and asked, "Is the treatment just a formula that would be essentially the same in any location? Will they do exactly the same treatment in Tahoe that you would have prescribed? Do you know anyone up here? What kind of reputation does this cancer center have?" The treatment looked a lot like a recipe in my mind, and if that were true, where it was administered didn't matter.

Josh not only reassured me that the treatment would be the same but, above and beyond that, told me that he had a home in Truckee and would check out the cancer center on his next trip. Strangely, when I went to my first oncology appointment in Tahoe, Josh was standing in the lobby, waiting to meet with the director and to have a tour of the facility. During his research of the facility, he realized that the director had been a colleague of his at the David Geffen School of Medicine at UCLA. He later called to assure me that I would be well taken care of if I decided to have treatment in Tahoe. After hearing that, I breathed a huge sigh of relief and felt as if I was in good hands. There was no longer any doubt in my mind that I would go through chemo and radiation locally.

By then I had also learned that the cancer center was affiliated with the University of California at Davis and had a knowledgeable staff and group of physicians who simply wanted to practice in an idyllic location. Hard to blame them. The medical staff had weekly video conferences with Davis, so I had the benefit of a university medical center and the beauty of a mountain town with sophisticated medical personnel and a state-of-the-art cancer center, all packaged into one. Although my decision had already been made, this was further confirmation that my choice was the right one for me. The last thing I wanted was to have to travel to the Bay Area for chemo and radiation in addition to the business trips I would already be taking to San Francisco. In hindsight, I am somewhat embarrassed that I assumed a big-city cancer center would be vastly superior to the local center. I never looked back and am grateful I made the choice to receive my treatment at my local center. The professional and thoughtful treatment was the baseline, and the spa-like environment was a bonus, one that I appreciated in the coming months and years.

CHAPTER 20

Cancer FREEBIES

THE SUPPORT PROVIDED BY THE cancer center was far beyond my expectations, so I didn't seek any outside support. I should have, if for no other reason than that I would have found out about the creative arts programs, which sound like a lot of fun. There were tons of benefits that I only discovered after my treatment. Just recently, I took my puppy for an interview at doggy day care. I had found out just by chance that the facility offers to take in dogs of cancer patients while they are undergoing treatment. While my dog demonstrated how she could play well with others at this version of dog heaven (with a swimming pool just for the dogs and four play yards), I mentioned to the owner how wonderful I thought it was that she extended this offer. She just smiled and replied: "Two-time survivor, bilateral mastectomy." I mention this not only because I encourage you to look for these types of unique resources that may exist in your area but also as an example of the thousands of people who have been through cancer and will do all they can to help you through it.

This incident prompted me to do more research on cancer perks. In addition to the ones that I knew about and took advantage of at the cancer center, I discovered organizations that offer biofeedback; telecom counseling; online exercise programs; peer navigator programs; caregiver education and navigation workshops; deep relaxation; a wig bank; and even a class to make "SoulCollage," cards featuring collages reflecting an aspect of your personality or soul. There are other creative arts offered to cancer patients, including writing, dance, and music. Some of these things sound so enticing that it seems a shame that they are only offered to cancer patients.

Research for benefits offered nationally uncovered all kinds of financial help, including food assistance programs, payment of monthly utility bills, assistance in navigating insurance and/or Medicare, taxi vouchers, gasoline cards, bridge tolls, metro passes and van services, and payment of rent and mortgage expenses. Angel Flight America provides air transportation assistance. My favorite was a group that buys Christmas presents for families battling cancer who would not otherwise be able to afford them. There are children's services; oncology social workers; free personal and private blogs and websites to connect family and friends during a health challenge; videos for children about cancer; Reiki; Tai Chi; horticulture therapy; and assistance with housecleaning, medical equipment, and prostheses. If you live in East Tennessee, you can even get a free recliner from the United Cancer Support Foundation!

I provide you with this preliminary laundry list to give you ideas about what to look for and ask for during your cancer treatment. Look locally and nationally and take full advantage of the services that you are able to uncover. You will find a wide network of groups, organizations, and individuals that want to help you and who are trained to fully understand your experience.

CHAPTER 21

POST-SURGICAL *Treatment*

Chemo

Given my lack of interest in medical research on cancer, I had only a very general idea of exactly what chemo was intended to accomplish as I was going through it—apart from the broad-brush goal of curing cancer. It wasn't until I started writing this book that I had a more scientific interest in how and what it did. I did an Internet search and learned that chemotherapy is supposed to halt the division of cancer cells, which characteristically have no checks and balances in place to control and limit cell division. Usually, the chemotherapy drugs work by damaging the RNA or DNA that tells the cell how to copy itself in division. If the cells are unable to divide, they die. Chemo is most effective at killing cells that are rapidly dividing, but it can't otherwise distinguish between normal cells and cancerous cells. The normal cells will grow back and be healthy, but the interim damage is what leads to typical side effects, such as hair loss, nausea, and low blood cell count. The frequency and type of chemo is based on the type of cancerous cells found and the rate at which they divide. I found all of this weirdly fascinating.

A typical chemo treatment for me involved packing up some work to keep me occupied for a few hours and heading out the door to the "cancer spa." During the infusions of Taxotere and Cytoxan, I would look up often enough to acknowledge the IV and confirm my name and birth date. Taxotere and Cytoxan were the drugs designed to attack the type of cancer I had. I went for chemo every three weeks for a total of five treatments. A typical treatment lasted four to five hours, which gave me plenty of time to catch up on work.

Although work was my distraction during cancer treatments, I can't recommend highly enough that you stay busy on your own terms. When I say "on your own terms," I mean that whatever you take on as your distraction needs to be just that, not a burden. I don't recommend distractions that require you to be at a certain place at a certain time; you may not feel like doing whatever it is you signed up for when the time comes. For the same reason, I don't recommend anything that others are relying on you to get done. Whether it's tackling those books on your nightstand that you never have time to read, going to yoga classes for cancer patients, knitting sweaters for your entire family, updating your Christmas card list, organizing your photos, or even catching up on a few Netflix series—stay busy. Every minute that your mind remains unoccupied is a minute that it may drift to negative thoughts, which I guarantee are not going to help you.

Between work projects at my chemo sessions, I occasionally had time to talk with the nurses. Once during a session, one of my nurses, Stephanie, asked, "Are you local?"

"Just barely," I responded, knowing intuitively that a former Bay Area resident would never really be considered local in this community, at least not until they had endured a few rough winters. At this point, I still had a few pairs of high heels in my closet and drove a Prius. I did not want to risk the gales of hilarity that might be caused were I to claim local status.

"I was diagnosed with cancer on the day we moved here from the Bay Area," I offered.

"Wow, that sucks. How do you like it here?" Stephanie asked.

"Except for the cancer thing, I love it! When I leave my house to run errands, I can't believe how lucky I am to live someplace this beautiful."

"What kind of work do you do?" Stephanie inquired as she studied my briefcase.

"Real estate law," I responded. "My office is still in San Francisco, but I work remotely most of the time. In fact, I have a crapload of work that I'm hoping to get through while I'm sitting around here."

"Okay, we'll just start up the IV, and you let us know if you need anything."

"Will do," I replied.

Stephanie understood and assured me that I would have privacy in my little alcove before excusing herself to tend to the official business of administering the chemo drugs. I turned off my phone, put an out-of-office response on my email, and focused on the paperwork in front of me. I was not going to be that person making self-important phone calls when others were trying to relax.

A couple of hours later, I asked an important logistical question. "I have to go to the bathroom. Do I just wheel the IV in there?"

"Yes, we'll help you with that," Stephanie said.

When I got to the bathroom, I noticed that a big sign was posted with the instruction to flush twice. My memory of the sign transformed this innocuous wording into a large sign with a skull and crossbones and the wording "Warning, chemo is poison," or something to that effect. When I recently went back to the chemo room on one of my follow-up appointments, I asked if I could go in and take a look at the sign. All it said was "If you are undergoing chemo, flush twice." Funny how the mind works. I do remember that I asked one of the nurses why that sign was posted, and again, I'm certain that my memory is more graphic than the reality, but my recollection is that she said, "The chemo going through your body is poison, and the sign is there to protect others from exposure to that poison."

She probably couched her response in softer terms, but in any event, the whole idea that I was being treated with poison was a pretty big eye-opener. As I said earlier, the scientific precision of cancer treatment was new and intriguing to me. Now that I was undergoing treatment, I was focused on an entirely different aspect of cancer. Before I was diagnosed, I felt great. It was only after the treatment began that I had any sense of being sick. So, unlike my other medical experiences, the cure felt a lot worse than the disease.

At the end of the first treatment, Stephanie confirmed my next appointment. "Hmm, three weeks from now. By then, your hair will have fallen out," she said matter-of-factly. Initially, I was horrified that anyone could refer to this event so nonchalantly. Then, braced with my newfound mantra—*I do not define myself by my hair*—I accepted the comment at face value and did not dwell on it.

For the chemo treatments, I always went solo, as I had decided to do at the outset. This was not for lack of caring by my friends and family but rather because I always took my laptop and a pile of documents to go through. Anyone who volunteered for the handholding-during-chemo role was politely refused. I didn't want to make them feel as if there was no way to help, but I needed to stay focused on work. My cancer treatment took place at a busy time in the California real estate market, so I just kept working whenever I could. In fact, work was a phenomenal distraction from the cancer crisis looming in the background, and it fit with the denial approach that I had adopted early on. During chemo, I enjoyed four to five hours of work time with few interruptions. The fire pit warmed the entire room. During the winter, I could watch the snow fall out the window while staying nice and toasty. As far as chemo treatments went, it wasn't half bad.

One day, I decided to try acupuncture during a chemo treatment, just to see whether it would make a difference. Since my side effects from chemo were minor, it was difficult to tell, but the acupuncturist was a nice guy, so I told him that it was "great, really helpful." In actuality, I felt a little jumpy and had a hard time sitting still, which is important when you have needles inserted all over your body. Since the benefit in my case was minimal, I decided to forgo the acupuncture for future treatments.

I don't want to imply that chemo was a breeze, but it was certainly a lot easier than I had anticipated. Again, the science and precision were awe-inspiring. Prior to treatment, I was given a host of medications to ward off any unpleasant side effects, including four levels of nausea medications to use depending on the severity of the nausea. Since I don't really enjoy puking and am generally not good at following directions, I just went to the highest level right off the bat, and that seemed to do the trick.

Neutropenia

Since undergoing chemo, "neutropenia" has become part of my new vocabulary. In layman's terms, it's when your white blood cells plummet to nothing, and you risk "leaving the building" early from any or every infection under the sun. "Has Elvis left the building?" has always been one of my favorite euphemisms for an untimely demise. But if that's too vernacular, the dictionary definition of neutropenia states that "it is an undesirable side effect of some cancer treatments." I can attest to the accuracy of this definition.

Although my first round of chemo went fine, I had a history of muscle and bone pain that was just sitting around waiting for me to stir things up. Unfortunately, I succeeded, and it showed up in spades after my first treatment. Neulasta is an injection given the day after chemo to boost your white cell count, which is often decimated by the chemo. Neulasta can cause muscle and bone pain, even if you do not have a predisposition to that. So, for me, it was almost predictable. My oncologist Nancy was sympathetic to the muscle and bone pain I experienced following the first chemo treatment and asked if I would consider going without Neulasta the next time around, since my blood cell count looked good after the first one.

"Why not?" I said and went for it.

Five to nine days after a chemo treatment, a blood test is done to determine whether the blood cell counts are at a healthy level. The blood tests after the second round of chemo without the Neulasta, however, showed that I had scary-low levels of white blood cells. Nancy had warned me of the risks of skipping the injection, so I was aware of the possibility of a drop in white blood cells, which are the gatekeepers between you and infection. When she saw the results of the blood tests, however, she looked me in the eye and said, "I don't know how to say this, but you could die from this if you get an infection that is not treated right away." Again, I thought it was nice of her to share, but I still had a stash of denial at my fingertips to convince me that nothing bad would happen. I did, however, appreciate the gravity of the warning, and although the information sunk in, I didn't foresee that it would have too much of an impact on my life.

I left her office with a firm understanding that if I had a fever above 101.4, I should go straight to the ER. I was also told to stay out of crowds and to take lots of other precautions to avoid exposure to infection. I'm not always perfect at following instructions, but clearly, she meant business, hence the blunt warning.

After my appointment, I went home and went back to work. It was late on a Friday afternoon, so after I finished up a conference call, I decided to call it a day. I was cold, so I tucked myself into

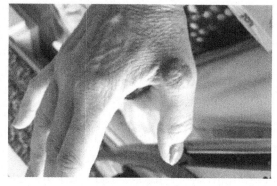

Suspicious paper cut

bed to warm up a little. I noticed that I had a mild fever of about 99. Since my days are filled with shuffling my own paper around the house, I am prone to paper cuts. That week was no exception, and I had gotten a paper cut or two. Later that afternoon, the paper cuts were looking suspicious and really started to hurt. *This is the infection that could kill me,* I thought. I finally dismissed the idea that Nancy's warnings were just talk. The irony of dying from a paper cut after all the medical challenges I had faced in my life did not escape me.

In no time, my fever was up, and when it got to 101.4, my husband rushed me to the hospital. By the time we got to the ER, which was only ten minutes away, my fever was up to 103. A few powerful antibiotics later, I was feeling pretty good, and within a very short time the fever was down. As a precaution, I was checked into the hospital.

Apparently, once you set off the neutropenia alarms, you don't get to go home right away. As the nurse explained it, "We just need to watch your white blood cell count until it comes up to five hundred or so." Loving a challenge, I wanted a yardstick to tell me what that meant in percentage terms and how far I had left to go to get to five hundred.

Curious, I asked, "What is it now?"

The nurse said, "Well, right now, you're at zero."

I'm sure my face visibly fell as any sense of entertainment from the prospect of a numeric challenge was obliterated. At this point, I thought I was in the hospital for the long haul. However, I had been down this road before, and I appreciated the private rooms and the personal attention that you get at a twenty-four-bed hospital, instead of one with hundreds of patients. Bob hung around for a while, but once I convinced him I was fine and we just had to wait it out until the antibiotics took their full effect, he went home to get my laptop, my phone, and some of his own paperwork to keep him busy while he kept me company.

There are a couple of things I distinctly remember about that three-day hospital stay. First was mealtime. The food service people gleefully brought me breakfast. I was just surveying the spread, which again was shockingly good, from the same hospital restaurant that served up the gourmet lunches for chemo patients. I was appreciative of the meals they served me, because I'd been in enough hospitals to know that yummy hospital food was a rare exception.

Just as I was about to shovel in the first spoonful of steel-cut oatmeal with berries, the nurse swooped in and snatched the entire tray away from me. I was a little taken aback at the aggressiveness of the move, until she informed me that I was so vulnerable to infection that I couldn't eat fresh fruit or vegetables. Instead, my diet was to consist of more uniformly sterilized foods, like canned peaches in sugary high-fructose corn syrup. I had been struggling to learn healthier eating habits at the encouragement of my daughters—whom I affectionately referred to as the food police. So, even a brief interlude with processed, decidedly un-fresh food was anathema to me. I got through it, and really, it was a little bit of a 1960s flashback. Remember Kraft Macaroni & Cheese? When I was in college, it was twenty-nine cents a box. At that time, I lived on the stuff and thought I was eating right. During my hospital stay, I returned to my dietary roots, which was simultaneously challenging and comforting.

The other memory I have from that hospital stay is that, since I felt pretty good as soon as the antibiotics kicked in, I didn't see any reason why I shouldn't be catching up on the work that was piling up, provided I was extra careful with the paper, of course. Once Bob brought me my phone and computer, for all the legal world knew, I was "in the office." The nurses were so accommodating that they agreed to put a Post-it on my door to keep people out when I was on conference calls. I have no idea if they remember me, or if I stood out among their patients, but I will always remember them for their kindness and flexibility.

Fortunately, my remaining three chemo treatments went smoothly, followed by Neulasta. For some reason, the bone and muscle pain I had experienced from the first round of chemo with Neulasta was minor in the later rounds. There was even a very cool form of the drug that was being tried out, for which I volunteered to be a guinea pig. A little disc with the Neulasta was taped onto my stomach, and the disc released the drug on its own via built-in injection roughly twenty-four hours after chemo. Sometimes, it was hard for me to come back to the cancer center the next day for the injection, so this experiment had my name written all over it. I'm happy to report that it worked great, without a hitch.

The chemo nurses at the center deserve special attention. Around Halloween, we talked about their kids' costumes. One nurse was expressing consternation that her two-year-old boy wanted to dress as a woman. We all convinced her that it was too early for her to read anything into it, and even if the little tyke grew up to be a cross-dresser, that was out of her control. Then they asked if I was going to dress up for Halloween.

"Probably not," I responded, since I didn't have kids living at home and our neighborhood didn't attract a lot of trick-or-treaters. As I thought further, though, I offered that maybe I could just take off my wig and go to the downtown Truckee celebration as "The Scream."

I also remember being in the chemo room one day when one of the nurses received a phone call, which brought a huge smile to her face and tears to her eyes. She was finally able to announce her first pregnancy to the others on staff. There wasn't a dry eye around as it was a very emotional and endearing moment. Witnessing that connection to their lives outside of work made me feel as if I belonged there on some level. I would be embarrassed if I learned that they didn't remember me, when they had meant so much to me during my treatments. At a follow-up appointment recently, I discovered my worry was unwarranted. One of the nurses asked how things were going and "did I need to rent out one of the chemo chairs to get some work done?" They remembered me all right. I was thrilled to know that I was not just a number on a chart and that I had left a lasting impression.

Radiation

Having grown up in Los Angeles and having lived most of my life in the Bay Area, I was new to the mountains and was clueless about how to drive in the snow. As the treatments progressed into late fall, the first snow fell, and my impromptu lessons began. I'm proud to report that I drove myself to and from my appointments, with only one weather-related mishap that happened when another driver skidded in the ice and broadsided me, just a little.

I have been chastised at times for referring to Truckee as a small town, but after Bob got home from skiing that day, he mentioned that the shuttle driver said he'd swerved to avoid five different accidents, and that he'd seen one collision involving a woman in a Mercedes. A few months later, our neighbor was selling an outdoor chair and asked if I could show it to a woman who was interested.

"Of course, just send me her name, and I'll call her," I texted her back.

The woman who wanted the chair turned out to be my oncologist Nancy. When she ended up buying the chair, we loaded it in her car. She apologized for driving such an old beater but said that it was a rental car. Her Mercedes had been in the shop for weeks after she was T-boned in the intersection near our homes, she explained. A light bulb went on, and I asked her when that had happened. We put the pieces together and realized that her car was the Mercedes that the shuttle driver was referring to, and that we had both gotten hit in the same intersection on the same day, because of the same patch of ice. So, when I say Truckee is a small town, it is not small in the sense of being unsophisticated, but it's small enough to guarantee that once you've lived there for a couple of years, you will constantly cross paths with the people you've met. Because of this dynamic, I no longer honk at bad drivers, nor do I use any hand signals to advise other drivers that they have offended me. The other driver is more likely than not someone I know.

I did not need to drive to my appointments if I chose not to do so. The American Cancer Society has a program to drive you to appointments, if you need it. Again, this was in one of the brochures I didn't read. I'm putting it here, in case someone else can benefit from it. For my daily radiation appointments, I didn't flinch at a little snow falling. I am neurotic about keeping appointments and try my best to be on time. Had I appreciated the risks of driving in inclement weather, I might have canceled some appointments, but I never canceled a single one. The staff was often surprised when I showed up even when the weather was bad. I'm not saying I was incredibly brave. I think it was more that I was incredibly ignorant about the risks of driving in the ice and snow. By the way, the car that I used to trudge through the snow was a Prius with snow tires. You don't see many Priuses in the mountains, for reasons that became apparent to me when Bob was driving the car one day, and it got stuck in snow entering our driveway. The car sat there like a teeter-totter until a friend could come and help Bob pull it out.

✳ ✳ ✳

The radiation room is, by necessity, a little cold and daunting. Upon arriving, I was asked to change into a gown. There was a jigsaw puzzle in the radiation waiting room, and I was disappointed that I was never left there long enough to find a single piece to the puzzle. The radiation room door—which is about two feet thick—had a "Danger" sign that displayed a skull and crossbones. This time, I am certain the sign had dire warnings and was not just a product of my imagination. The table you lie on for the treatment is the same as for any X-ray: metallic, cold, hard, and uncomfortable. The radiation is administered from inside a control room, isolating the techs from the patient and the radiation.

I don't remember a lot about the radiation treatments except that they were short. Before the first one, coordinates were charted so that the radiation was focused in the same spot every time. To mark those coordinates, you got little pinpoint tattoos, one in the middle and one on each side. I had always threatened my daughters that if they wanted to get a tattoo, I would too. I wrongly figured that this was a creative deterrent. These little dots were not what I had envisioned when I'd made the threat.

For the actual treatment, I was asked to hold my breath for a few seconds while they zapped me, and that was it. Done. Ten minutes start to finish and not uncomfortable in the least. Again, I could probably tell you more about the people administering the treatment than I could about the actual treatment. I learned all about their favorite bars and restaurants in the area. One of the women had just gotten engaged, so there was a lot to talk about, and I appreciated the distraction.

Outside the radiation room, there was a little bell on the wall. When leaving your last radiation appointment, the staff would ring the bell, and you'd go through a small reception line to the cheers, hoots, and hollers of the assembled group. It's a hokey little tradition, but it forces you to smile and be a little silly on your way out the door. When it was my turn, had I not already been in celebration mode, the bell was also a reminder that something good had just happened. I had just completed the active phases of my treatment and did a dorky little dance on my way through the reception line. The next step was being on the road to feeling better and getting back to a normal life.

PART SIX:

The Support

CHAPTER 22

LEAN *on* ME

I WOULD BE REMISS IN discussing my treatment if I didn't also describe the support group that helped me through it. This is also where I hope to fulfill my promise to help you with saying or doing the right thing for a cancer patient, by offering you examples of the right things and a couple of very wrong things. I have never been to a traditional support group, which I understand to be a gathering of strangers with similar issues. Instead, my support group consisted of my family and a dog or two, along with some friends and business colleagues. Some were aware of their roles; others participated in equally significant ways, unknowingly.

Jenny and Friends

While our kids were growing up, Jenny and I had coffee, got dinner, and occasionally went for walks with a gang of moms and dogs in the neighborhood. However, we never had enough one-on-one time to develop the relationship that we have today. Once all of our kids were off to college, our relationship had the chance to evolve in a way that we never had the time or the attention span for when we were occupied with school, sports, and school-and-sports-related social activities.

Jenny's involvement in my story is just one of the reasons that our relationship has grown. Now that our kids are launched on their own paths, and though we no longer live close enough to go for morning walks or have a cup of coffee together, Jenny and I have reconnected, and our friendship is stronger than ever. Often when I visit the Bay Area, I stay at Jenny's house (with the screeching cat) or we have dinner together. It is because of her that my cancer was detected so early and that I had a top-notch team working to help me fight it. For that I will always be grateful.

I met a new friend in the exercise classes at our new community who offered what I will call "silent support." When I showed up for the classes wearing a scarf, she didn't ask a single question. She is one of those people who feels deeply, has been through more than her share of shitshows, and waits patiently for you to offer up your story if and when you choose to do so. Even if I had decided to keep everything to myself, she still would have welcomed me as a friend. She offered exactly what I needed in our new location, although I couldn't have told you that at the time.

So many other friends came out of the woodwork to share their cancer stories or a friend's or relative's cancer story, none of which I had ever heard about before my friends became aware of my experience with cancer. It turned out that one new friend from the Lake Tahoe community had been treated by my oncologist Josh for melanoma years ago and had very fond memories of him, his compassion as a doctor, and his professional treatment. The fact that she had melanoma several years ago and is still around speaks for itself.

My Colleagues

Because I invested a lot of time and energy in my work while I had cancer, many of my colleagues and business contacts became part of my support group. I have been a lawyer in private practice for the past thirty-seven years. After the first thirty-four years, I finally landed at a law firm that was my life dream. I actually designed a law firm in my imagination similar to where I worked and was stupefied when I found it actually existed. This is what is known in the legal field as a "boutique" firm—one that focuses on certain specialties. In our case, it was real estate.

The founders of this firm are women, and most, but not all, of the partners are women. We qualify for work that public entities can only give to firms that meet certain criteria for women-owned firms. Most of the partners are large-firm refugees seeking more flexibility than those firms offered. As money was not wasted on elaborate office space, the firm offers the option to work in the office or remotely. The two named partners actually worked from cubicles when they were in the office. Most of the other attorneys shared offices.

The interview with this firm was, in my mind, epic. Beyond the "we don't care if you work from the moon" comment (of which I took full advantage by moving to Lake Tahoe), one of the other quotes that I will always remember is "we will *never* have video conferencing." I thought this was odd, since we were at the technological forefront of the industry, a stone's throw from Silicon Valley. So, of course, I asked why. They all laughed and said, "Obviously, because we're usually in our Lulus and jammies when we work from home." You can see why I loved this firm after coming from more traditional law firms. I smiled, already knowing that I wanted to work there, and this was just one more reason.

At another point during the same interview, sweat started pouring down my face. I was concerned that they might think I was nervous, which really wasn't the case. I was having a great time. So, I just volunteered why I was pouring sweat: "Forgive me; I'm having a hot flash." I think that was the moment they decided to hire me. There were, of course, professional reasons to hire me as well, but this seemed to tip the scales. My practice area was a real estate niche that fit in perfectly with their broader real estate practice. I had clients who were similar to theirs, and I provided an expertise that their clients frequently needed, and which the firm had previously been farming out to other law firms that specialized in the type of work I did. For me, the opportunity to work for their clients as well as mine was enticing. For them, they could now keep this work in-house instead of introducing their clients to other law firms, which is something law firms hate to do. In addition to the professional motivations, we all had a good laugh over the hot flash.

As we talked, I felt that I had known these women for ages and that we shared the same goals and philosophies. When they extended an offer, there was no question I would accept it. I waited a couple of days so I wouldn't appear overanxious, but then I called to say how excited I was to have the opportunity to join their firm.

During my cancer treatment, these same work colleagues, and even my clients, provided me with a support network, although I'm sure most of them didn't realize it. A couple of pivotal events come to mind. After the move to Lake Tahoe, I worked remotely most of the time, which worked great. However, I still visited San Francisco frequently for client meetings, just to stay in touch and attend law firm meetings.

When we first moved, I usually stayed with either Jenny or Susan, one of my law partners. In her spare time, Susan fosters dogs and often had quite an array of characters in residence. The one-pound Chihuahua comes to mind, along with the blind Dalmatian and some others. The Chihuahua was shaking in his tiny boots when he first arrived on the scene. As only a small dog can, he soon made his presence and personality known, demanding attention and cuddling up with anyone who would have him. He was a heartbreaker, so much so that Susan's mom ended up adopting him. To this day, they are a team.

The blind Dalmatian spent the first few days in the house crashing into walls and furniture but quickly figured out the lay of the land and gracefully made his way through the house. A single man who needed him as much as the Dalmatian needed a home eventually adopted him. In addition to the foster animals, Susan had multiple pets of her own. There was no way to disrupt a household like this, so I never felt that I was an imposition. The house was somewhat of a menagerie and had a certain chaos to which I could neither add nor detract.

On one of these visits, Susan and I were sharing a glass of wine when I came to the horrendous realization that I had left my wig, Jen, up in Tahoe. At this stage, my hair was about a quarter inch long and, once again, newly red. We had a scheduled client visit and a project tour the next day. Driving back to Tahoe to fetch Jen was not realistic. So, I tried to buck up and face the music. I immediately said, "Susan, another glass of wine, please. I forgot my wig." She dutifully complied. We then surveyed the options and concluded that I just had to forge ahead, wigless.

The next day, we showed up for the client meeting and project tour. When we walked into one of the model homes at my client's project, several members of the sales team, client team, and others were assembled in a meeting. People visibly gasped when they saw me, then tried to conceal their shock. I would have done the same. Many of those assembled did not even know that I had cancer, so the surprise element was huge. Consistent with the plan Susan and I had laid out, I ignored all the reactions. Later, I found out that the conversation had gone something like "What the hell happened to her?" as soon as I left the room. I admit that I was pleased with

Me, realizing that I forgot my wig

myself for leaving all of this to their imagination. Unless they asked me a direct question, I was not going to offer up any information or explanations. In my mind, it reflected the highest level of professionalism I had ever been able to muster and for which I was quite proud. I was also happy to have to leave the room for the tour of the project before my attempt at professionalism imploded.

For client meetings, my go-to outfit consisted of a work dress, tights, and (hopefully fashionable) shoes. The tights turned out to be the icing on the cake for the day of the wigless project tour. Now that I was up in Tahoe, I didn't wear tights very often. In the course of the tour, I discovered that my tights, which had sat in my drawer for over a year, had lost their elastic. The elevator in the project was occupied by the workers finishing the final details of the project. That meant that we clambered up the stairs of a several-story condo project, during which the elastic in my tights gave way entirely. After a few flights of stairs, my tights were pooled around my ankles. The only thing I could do was stop midway on the stairs, take off my shoes, and remove my tights, which I tried to do discreetly. Others probably noticed, including some of the construction workers. In any case, I stuffed the tights in my purse and continued on. That day set new standards for what constituted a bad hair day and wardrobe malfunctions. More importantly, it set new standards for what could happen to my appearance without me caring one way or the other.

A final note on the impact of my business connections during this time. A touching surprise happened at a business lunch with a woman I had worked with for almost twenty years on many projects. Over the years, we had become friends as much as we were business colleagues. We frequently scheduled lunches to vent our frustrations and check in on each other's lives. She had a reputation as a tough, no-nonsense businesswoman with a bit of a sharp bite. When I told her I had cancer, she cried. Her reaction was another thing I did not see coming but which touched me deeply.

My Family

My family has already been introduced to you in passing. I will try to zero in on the essence of who they are and how they provided the unique support that I wanted and needed during my treatment.

Bob

Bob and I both love sports, travel, and the outdoors. We had good careers, had traveled extensively, and by the time we met, had kissed enough frogs to know a prince or princess when we found one. I have a couple of theories about our dynamic. Bob stabilizes me. I'm the person who bought a home on a shoe-shopping trip. Over the course of my lifetime, I have been known to do other impulsive things, too many to count. Bob is more pragmatic. While Bob is math and science, I am literary. Bob has an undergraduate electrical engineering degree and an MBA, and I majored in comparative literature in college. I went to Berkeley. He went to Stanford. We are not out of the same mold. Instead, we complement each other.

We had children late in life, meaning we were old enough to be AARP members shortly after our kids were born. We were part of that rare demographic that benefits from old-age privileges while having toddlers. There wasn't a single minute when we were raising our children where either one of us thought we were missing out on anything. We had had the opportunity during our single years for lots of adventures, but raising children was the richest and best experience of our lives.

In the teenage years, all hell broke loose. Our formerly angelic children, their friends, and their acquaintances were trailblazing in ways we never anticipated. Had we been honest with ourselves, we may have recalled that our teenage years involved a little bit of hellraising too, but viewing it from the other side is much more frightening. Somehow, we limped through those years and shipped the kids off to college, much to the collective relief of both parents and children.

When I was diagnosed with cancer, Bob was there in whatever capacity I needed. But what I needed was not typical. We had a long-planned sailing trip to Croatia on the books when my cancer treatment intervened. We had just decided to cancel the trip when our daughter Kelly walked into the room and volunteered: "If Mom can't go, I'll go."

"No way," Bob said. "Mom's chemo starts a few weeks before the trip, and she needs us with her." We still had no idea how chemo would affect me. So, I suggested that they plan the trip, and if I needed them to cancel it at the last minute, so be it.

The first chemo treatment went fine, except for that one day in bed with the muscle and bone aches and pains, so I pushed them out the door. I assured them that I could call on my mom, sister, and friends for any help that I needed. In the meantime, Bob had an opportunity to spend two weeks with his nineteen-year-old daughter who was about to leave for college. The trip was a flotilla, meaning that an organizer gets a group together, and they set off on a few sailboats, following roughly the same itinerary. They had a blast! The trip became a food and wine excursion through the islands off the Dalmatian Coast of Croatia, which was right in Kelly's wheelhouse.

Our Daughters

Bob and I love our children happily, intensely, and painfully. We have been so tremendously lucky. Both girls are beautiful, inside and out, in very different ways. Both have asked me what their defining moment was in life.

"When did you first see what I would become?"

One answer is "on the day you were born." One daughter was mellow and sleepy, the other alert, checking out her surroundings with a ferocity that was somewhat alarming in a newborn.

The more definitive answer for Ren was "the first day of kindergarten."

We arrived at the classroom where all the kids and parents were lined up outside the door, with most of the kids clutching their parents' hands for life. Ren left our side and went up and down the line introducing herself to all the kids. As she approached one child who was not interacting with the other kids and who Ren deduced was Hispanic, she said, "Hola, me llamo Lauren." (We had a Spanish-speaking nanny at the time who had taught her some Spanish.) The two children chatted in Spanish, and soon after, the shy girl had her first kindergarten friend. That day, Ren sparked many new friendships, and it was clear that she had a gift for connecting with and caring deeply about people.

***

Later that year, we began on our Christmas Eve tradition, which consisted of a circuit around Union Square to see the oversized Christmas tree, take a look at the puppies and kittens in the window at Macy's, and make a stop at FAO Schwarz so they could each pick out one toy. We then wandered over to the St. Francis hotel and had hors d'oeuvres and lots of father-daughter dances as the band played in the hotel restaurant. This had become one of our favorite family traditions. By the time Ren was five, we had added to the tradition, handing her a stack of dollar bills that she could give to those in need on our walk. She just couldn't make it around the block and enjoy all the lighthearted Christmas cheer when others were so much less fortunate. Her path of altruism was clear, even at that age. She would later go on to donate countless hours to help those in need. Her career path has led her to body therapy, yoga, nutrition, and craniosacral therapy as proactive measures against health problems.

For Kelly, the defining moment came when she was three. I was at her Montessori preschool one day, just watching. Kelly was in front of some cubbies when the kids were released to select from a variety of jobs. Kelly chose her job, but before she could get started, she had a line of five-year-olds behind her, anxiously waiting for Kelly to teach them their jobs. Kelly was, in essence, the manager. When I later read Sheryl Sandberg's book *Lean In*, I laughed at the comments from her brothers who said something to the effect that "she often treated us not as siblings but as her first employees." That was Kelly.

Kelly was born with a sophisticated palate. I was never able to get away with serving her milk one day past the expiration date. As a toddler, her favorite foods included clams and sushi. I didn't know at the time that it was a bad idea for a toddler to be eating sushi. When she was two, my mom and her husband were visiting. They came across her in the early morning on the floor of the kitchen, scrambling eggs in a bowl. She then hopped onto the couch, where she could reach over the top of the stove and cook them herself, with supervision, of course. She has since worked in restaurants and food service, until recently when she observed that the industry calls for long hours and working evenings and week-ends when everyone else is out having fun. This is a long way of saying that Kelly was a foodie starting at the ridiculous age of two. Or maybe it started earlier, but the tendency was difficult to detect until she could talk and eat solid food.

At times in our relationship, Kelly is the mom, and I'm okay with that. She knows that I also refer to her as my OCD child. From the age of five, she kept a notebook in which she planned each birthday party, starting right after the previous year's party. Events were planned in ten-minute increments, the invitees were listed, the menu was determined (with recipes and a grocery list), and the invitation was designed. She was a born event planner and chef.

How did these polar-opposite personalities react to my cancer diagnosis and treatment? They supported me, fed me, nurtured me, and entertained me. Kelly sponsored a group for the Walk for Life cancer fundraiser at her university. She baked for the event and also persuaded her boyfriend's fraternity to participate. One of the fra-ternity members had just been diagnosed with cancer, so they were eager to join forces. Bob, Ren, and I all came to the event. Bob and I rushed to the swag table and got our "survivor" and "caregiver" T-shirts and picked up pins advertising those roles. And we all did a lap around the track as a family.

When Kelly and Bob left for Croatia, my daughter Ren stayed with me and cooked fabulously healthy meals until she had to go back to school. She was vegan at the time, so I had to stretch my normal eating habits to enjoy the vegan diet. Cashew cheese, tofu burgers, smoothies with a lot of green things in them, not to men-tion all the supplements and teas I had never heard of. She had always viewed food as an energy source and a means of warding off disease. As an accomplished track and cross-country star in high school, she was able to experience the immediate effects that the right food had on performance. Her coaches advised the team what to eat for breakfast before a race and when to eat it. As a result, she had a fine-tuned sense of food, albeit a very different one from Kelly's. She was not a vegan because it was trendy but rather because she had independently researched the impact of different kinds of food on your body and concluded that this was the best approach for her at the time.

Like her sister, the roots of her food preferences started early. She was the rare toddler who would choose broccoli over sugar every time. When she went trick or treating, she gave all her candy away to Kelly as soon as she got home. Kelly would eat most of Ren's candy and her own in one sitting, then go into what I refer to as a "sugar coma." When Ren has committed to a health plan or a particular diet, she never strays, even for just that one cookie or puffed pastry. Consequently, she was the perfect chef for me at a time when I needed to preserve all the strength I had and dig deep for some additional resources.

That Thanksgiving I was banned from the kitchen. Ren cooked the vegan dishes, Kelly cooked the haute cuisine, and my mom made the traditional stuff. She was not, however, allowed to serve up the cranberry sauce that stays in the shape of the can when you serve it. Kelly was cooking cranberries from scratch, which my mom and I didn't even recognize as an option. Another family, one that had been friends

Ren, me (and "Jen"), Kelly, and Bob,
Thanksgiving 2015

of Bob's for fifty years, joined us that year. They had a home nearby at Squaw Valley. Three generations of their family came, and the youngest held everyone's attention. Her family thinks we remember her because she ate so much that she barfed all over the table at the end of dinner, but we would never have remembered that detail if they hadn't reminded us. In reality, no one in our family had spent much time recently around toddlers, so we took turns keeping her out of harm's way in a home that was by no means childproof. She charmed each of us with her giggles and her smile.

The family wanted to contribute their fair share to dinner, of course, but most of the dishes were already spoken for. We asked them to bring the unique things that made up their family tradition, and it blended perfectly with ours. I lounged on the sofa that day while a most spectacular meal was prepared. Watching my mom and daughters working in the kitchen together was fantastic! In keeping with one of our Thanksgiving traditions, we all had Bloody Marys as the cooking progressed. Kelly delivered mine to me on the sofa. Not only can she cook; she also mixes a mean drink.

Me

I get that it seems strange to include myself in my support group, but think about it: If you're not cheering for your own team and if you don't know what you need and when you need it, all the support in the world will seem awkward and wrong. This is related to my belief that whatever support you provide to a cancer patient should be tailored to their needs and preferences. There is no standard formula.

I was alone when my hair fell out. I could not have predicted that this would be perfect for me. I was ecstatic that I didn't have to deal with anyone else's reaction to my new look, except me, on my terms. I avoided mirrors, kept busy, and saw friends and family when I wanted to.

I never took a picture of me entirely without hair, although I did take a picture of my hair entirely without me. My editor told me it was too graphic for the book, so you'll just have to use your imagination as to what two-thirds of a head of hair looks like on the bench of a shower. Except for the now-trendy Vin Diesel bald look that some men sport, along with Buddhist monks and Sinéad O'Connor, most people over thirty just look like they have cancer to me when they lose or shave their hair. I had no desire to imprint that image on my memory with a photograph. My hairstylist graciously offered to shave my head after most of my hair fell out. I couldn't stand the thought, though, so I rejected her offer and never did it. After the shower incident, about a third of my hair made a valiant attempt to cling to my scalp. So, I grabbed the scissors and chopped much of it off. It didn't look all bad. But my handiwork lasted less than a week before the rest of my hair followed suit, and I started wearing the funky hat, scarf, and wig things.

Self-inflicted emergency haircut

By the time Bob and Kelly returned, I was pretty comfortable wearing a wig and sleeping in the pink cap that they gave me at Wig 'N Out. It had never occurred to me that, without hair, your head gets cold. Bob would rub my head as if he were rubbing a genie for good luck, and I thought it was sweet. He and Kelly had made it back from their trip just in time for my neutropenia episode.

Laura

My sister, Laura, always provides support, usually in nonverbal ways. She might text me an adorable photo of her dog, Sunny, or send a cartoon that applies to at least one of our lives, or text an anecdote of something that happened that day. I can always rely on her to make me laugh, no matter how dreary the day. There are memories of our childhood that only we share, and usually they are in a secret language we've developed. I recall one instance when our secret code produced hilarious results. When we were growing up, our brother collected a lot of lizards. Laura and I have always loved lizards, but the alligator lizards would bite your finger, and you had to shake it really hard to get the lizard off.

When we were in college, Laura came to visit me with a boy-friend, Dan. After we drank him under the table while playing the most advanced video game of the time, Pong, Laura became embar-rassed at his lack of stamina. When she started to shake her finger hard enough to disengage an alligator lizard, I got the message loud and clear that Dan's days were numbered. Dan, of course, was not even aware that any communication had been made. Not only can Laura always crack me up, but she brought Sunny to visit at a crit-ical time in my cancer treatment. Sunny's virtues will be extolled in just a little bit, but for now I can just say that he was the dog who most contributed to my support during my treatment.

Mom, A.K.A. the Caregiver

From the moment I was first diagnosed, my mom wanted to be the caregiver. Not for the free massage, which I never even mentioned to her, but just to be a mom. She was living in Oregon at the time and couldn't wait to come visit while Bob and Kelly were in Croatia so she could help in every way possible. Her plane arrived on time. However, I waited and waited, and she didn't surface. Finally, I went to the airline desk and asked what the heck had they done with my mom. Minutes later, they rolled her out in a wheelchair! They shared that she had taken a tumble on the stairs while boarding the plane and had injured her ankle. Mom was terribly guilt-ridden about this, but she really could not get up off the couch for the next few days, so I took care of *her*. That was fine with me, as she was there for emotional support, and we talked incessantly, which was way more important to me than having someone around to fix me dinner. Besides, that's what takeout is for.

My Oncologists

I was lucky enough to have not one but two oncologists, with whom I am on a first-name basis. Of course, I knew Josh, my Bay Area oncologist, on a first-name basis before I knew him professionally in a doctor-patient relationship. Josh set me on track for my entire course of treatment, even though it wasn't done by him. He gave me confidence that I was getting the right care in the right place, and I will be forever grateful for that.

Nancy, my oncologist in Truckee, became a friend along the way. When I explained to her some of the unique but severe side effects that the estrogen-blocking hormone may have triggered or contributed to, I could see that she was upset on a personal level beyond the professional relationship. She commented: "You know that I think of you as much more than a patient but also as a friend." I *did* know that. Often the business portion of our appointments would take fifteen minutes, but we would spend the next twenty minutes talking as friends, about upcoming vacations, my daughters, life in Truckee, and other things that we had in common.

The Dogs

Everyone who has ever had a dog knows that they, too, are part of the family. Dogs were as much a part of my support group as my human family and friends, but since a dog offers such a different and special form of affection, they deserve their own section. I recently read an article in *Newsweek* about a group of scientists concluding that dogs have emotions. I hope they didn't spend a lot of time and money on this research, since it's pretty obvious to the rest of us.

My sister, Laura, and her family came to visit while Bob was in Croatia and I was undergoing chemo. Most of our conversation revolved around their dog, Sunny. Sunny has a lot of personality. He can provide emotional support that you didn't even know you needed. Even though I couldn't easily accept support from humans, Sunny knew

Sunny the caregiver

exactly what to do. Dogs gravitate toward the person in the room who needs them the most. Sunny acknowledged and accepted this responsibility as soon as he pranced in the door.

If there was any way that I could have cared for a dog at that phase in my life, I would have adopted a puppy in a heartbeat. We had lost our dog to cancer just a couple of months prior to the Tahoe move. I was desperate for the loyalty and unconditional love that a dog offers, even if it's difficult for me to admit that.

It's also hard to be without a dog in Truckee, because everyone else has one. So, I volunteered to dog-sit for a friend while Bob was in Croatia and I was undergoing treatment. I thought it would be great to have a dog that could bark its head off if anything or anyone approached the house while I was there alone. I also needed a nonjudgmental companion. For three days, I loved having my friend's dog, Kita, to keep me company. We went on long walks around the neighborhood and bonded while binge-watching *Nurse Jackie* on Netflix. Kita made herself right at home and slept at the foot of my bed. Probably because of chemo and an impaired immune system, I unfortunately found out I was allergic to dogs for the first time in my life. After about three days of coughing and sneezing all night and waking up with horrendously swollen eyes, I had to hand Kita off to another neighbor.

I put Kita in my car to drop her off at the neighbor's house. Kita's parents had handed her off to me in a hurry and without a leash, because they were in the midst of a crisis of their own. The husband was still hospitalized weeks after a fall from a golf cart, when he sustained life-threatening injuries. Frankly, Kita was extremely well-mannered and, under normal circumstances, didn't need a leash. But when we took walks, she would chase squirrels relentlessly. In a new community with a lot of construction going on, there were dumpsters everywhere. We could easily be diverted for an hour if a squirrel ran under a dumpster. Kita would circle the dumpster, waiting impatiently for the squirrel to come out and raise the white flag. It never happened as Kita had hoped. She also spent an inordinate amount of time staring wistfully into the trees, hoping

that one of the little crit-
ters would drop from the
sky. Dog life just doesn't
get better than that.

Well, during the hand-
off, we pulled into the
neighbor's driveway, and I
opened the door to let the
dog out. At that moment,
a squirrel fell off the side
of the house onto the

Kita waiting for a squirrel to
jump down from a tree

ground right in front of Kita, who was off-leash and could not be
restrained. Unfortunately, my hysteria did not put a damper on
Kita's spirits. A chase ensued between Kita and the squirrel. Kita
won and proudly presented me with her prize. I tried with my most
polished diplomatic skills to convince Kita to drop the squirrel.
Nothin' doin'. Finally, I took Kita, with the now-dead squirrel in her
mouth, straight to the neighbor's front door. Being a relatively new
resident, I had yet to meet this neighbor. But as soon as she opened
the door, I said, "Hi. Nice to meet you. Sorry about the squirrel
issue, but I couldn't convince the dog . . ."

My neighbor nodded and said, "Wait a second. I'll be right back."
She returned to the front door with a kitchen trash bag that she put
over the dog's head and voilà! Out popped the squirrel. I will always
have the highest regard for this woman's presence of mind and
resourcefulness. Apparently, this was not her first dog-squirrel rodeo.

Now, three years after my cancer treatment, I've finally taken
the plunge and gotten a new puppy. I couldn't be more excited.
Charlie is a yellow lab and might even be a relative of Sunny's. She
has an abundance of personality, loves to play in the snow and
water, and is petrified of bears. When we travel, we drop Charlie
off at Sunny's house.

At first, Sunny was leery of Charlie, the pipsqueak who was grabbing ahold of his leash and dragging him around the room. However, as Charlie became a little older, they became inseparable. Laura sends me dozens of photos where they appear to be purposely imitating each other. My cancer treatment has been over for some time, but I still find Charlie to be a tremendous support and companion. She gets me out for walks even in the most miserable storms and cracks me up every single day.

Sunny and Charlie

CHAPTER 23

"IT'S YOUR FAULT" *and* OTHER THINGS YOU *Probably Shouldn't Say* TO CANCER PATIENTS

BEYOND THE INNER CIRCLE OF the support group, there is everyone else. Some who are sincere but clumsy in their efforts to help, others who are gracious in everything they do or say, and then those who miss the mark entirely and leave much to be desired in the support category.

Whether it's cancer or another personal crisis, my tendency has been to expect the worst from acquaintances or even strangers. My lack of faith in human nature under these circumstances only increases my gratitude when people rise above my low expectations of them. I'm happy to report that, most of the time, people were incredibly kind to me. In fact, I can only recall two instances of bad behavior during my entire cancer treatment, one of which came from a doctor, who should have known better.

When reviewing my medical records, this doctor, whom I had seen for some non-cancer issue and who I assure you was not affiliated with the cancer spa, mused, "So, your first live birth was at age thirty-eight."

"Yes," I replied, thinking, *Of course, I like to think of my children as live birth 1 and live birth 2. It's so endearing.*

"And you drink alcohol?"

"Yup."

"About how many drinks a week would you say?"

"About five," I lied. I assume that most physicians double the estimate that a patient provides on this topic, and if I am correct about that, he would have done the math and arrived at about the right number.

"And it says here that you were on hormone replacement therapy after your hysterectomy?" he asked.

"Right again." This guy could read!

He then announced, "You know that, in your case, your cancer was caused by lifestyle factors, not genetics. So, it's basically your fault."

I can't relay my thoughts about this doctor without lapsing into profanity, which I promised not to do, so I will just say, "What a jerk!" It's true that I had children late in life, had hormone replacement therapy after my hysterectomy, drank wine, and had lived for many years in a "cancer cluster" in Marin County, which was long considered to have the highest rate of breast-cancer diagnoses in the world. All of these were apparently cancer-causing choices. But jeez, I got married late, which I attributed to fate rather than a conscious decision to increase my chances of getting cancer. I also had decided to have children after I got married, being fairly certain that I was not the first to make that *reckless* decision.

And yes, I used the Estradiol patch for several years as hormone replacement therapy on the advice and recommendation of

Dr. Bailey, who had witnessed firsthand my near-death experience from the botched hysterectomy. In her opinion, my introduction to menopause had been dramatic enough and did not need to be exacerbated by the added physical trauma of a hormonal crash. I had read of the increased cancer risk with hormone replacement but was convinced that Dr. Bailey had weighed the advantages and disadvantages and come to a reasoned decision. From my viewpoint, hormone replacement therapy was also critically necessary after menopause to avoid shrieking at my then-teenage children on a regular basis. As I learned, one of the drawbacks of having children late in life is that your hormonal fluctuations may coincide with those of your children. This can create a situation that is less than optimal for you, your children, or anyone within shouting distance.

I also may have heard that drinking wine can increase your cancer risk, but I admit that I was willing to take my chances on that one. I still drink wine, having decided a long time ago that I prefer to do things I enjoy rather than live to be one hundred while deferring all gratification. My rationale is that I do other things to stay healthy, and if I have one vice, so be it.

As for living in Marin County, during the nine years that I lived there, I was blissfully unaware of the "cancer cluster" characterization until Dr. Bailey and I discussed it when she first called with the bad news. With all these justifications for my behavior, no matter how weak, I didn't know what to do with the doctor's accusation that I was responsible for my cancer, so I discarded it and concluded that the doctor was a jerk for telling me this, even if it were true. My cancer may have been my fault, but I found the finger-pointing to be childish and unprofessional. To this day, I'm not sure of the benefit of placing blame on the patient.

Free to Speak My Mind

One odd phenomenon that I experienced in having cancer was the liberating feeling that I should not put up with this kind of crap from anyone. As a lawyer, I understood confrontation to be an integral part of my professional life. But, for some reason, which may be generational or just a personality flaw, I erred on the side of being nonconfrontational with respect to my personal interactions before I had cancer. When faced with an offensive human being, I felt that social conventions prevented me from airing my thoughts.

Cancer, however, produced an epiphany that gave me the freedom to speak my mind. The logic goes something like this: "I'm going through a bad experience. To gather my resources to maintain the strength I need to get through this, I need to be a little selfish and protective of my emotional well-being. Therefore, to be around me, you need to do the same. If not, I'm going to do all I can to make you wish you had never crossed my path." This feeling stayed with me even after my treatment was complete. I wondered, in retrospect, why I had ever tried to disguise valid thoughts and feelings just to exchange niceties with someone who did not have the same regard for me. What this translates to is that I would never, at this stage of my post-cancer life, let this doctor off the hook for being an insensitive lout. I would either (1) give this blowhard a piece of my mind or, at the very least, (2) walk out of his office never to return. Maybe both. At the time, I went with option two, the passive-aggressive approach, since I had concluded that this guy was beyond salvation.

After my encounter with him, I decided that if bedside manner is not a course taught in medical school, it should be, and perhaps patients should teach it. You might guess that I would happily volunteer for this role. My welcoming remarks for "Sensitivity Training 101" would be as follows:

"Now, my esteemed doctors, please be reminded that the accumulation of body parts that you treat is a human being with emotions. Yes, that's right, human beings have emotions, *just like dogs*," I would emphasize. "What you do and say—or don't say—can affect their well-being as much as any physical trauma. You may be one of those rare individuals who does not experience emotion. If so, this class has your name written all over it.

"We will teach you to recognize signs of emotional distress [show the class a video of a patient sobbing uncontrollably] and help you practice phrases that, even if you are insincere in their delivery, may give your patients something to grasp on to. In other words, you can *pretend* not to be the heartless SOB that you are, and that pretense may be beneficial to that accumulation of body parts that has come to you with a problem."

"Furthermore, when you have bad news to deliver, running and hiding is not an option. Here's an approach you might instead use: 'It's difficult to deliver this news, but you have [name the condition or disease]. I will tell you what to expect and as much information as I can about the disease, then give you time to ask me any questions that you might have.' Not so difficult, is it?"

✳ ✳ ✳

When my niece was born with Down syndrome, these basic tenets of communication were sadly broken. The doctors never told Laura anything about the condition of her child. Three days after my niece was born, a nurse blurted it out by accident. Everyone had suspected that something was wrong, but the added tension of not knowing was unnecessary. So, you see, even the *failure* to say something can alter a patient's perspective for the worst.

Fortunately, I have encountered many caring doctors, nurses, and other medical professionals in my cancer treatment, so I know that not all doctors suffer from this emotional handicap. On the positive side, the sometimes abominable behavior of an insensitive medical professional can shift your focus from the actual crisis.

Sadly, the second instance of substandard behavior that I experienced also involved a medical professional. In this case, it was a notorious pharmacist, Bud, in my new community. One day when I was waiting in line for one of the prescriptions from my oncologist—dressed in my scarf-hat thing, just in case he had any doubt that I was a cancer patient—I was rendered speechless for a moment when Bud blatantly skipped over me to wait on the attractive, much younger woman behind me.

By this time, the epiphany about not being treated like crap had already occurred to me. Stooping to the level of the rude pharmacist, I spoke up: "What am I? Invisible?"

Sensing an irate tirade in the making, Bud made the astute decision to wait on me. Then, as though we had been playing a game of "can you top this?" Bud looked at the prescription and said, "I can't honor this. I don't recognize this as being a signature. It's too simple to be a signature."

"What?!" I responded, beginning to sound somewhat shrill.

"You'll have to go back and get a new prescription from your doctor," he explained dispassionately. By this point, my nostrils were flaring, and I considered jumping over the counter to throttle this guy.

"Can't you just freaking call her?" I asked. "Do you really think cancer drugs are abused? I'm not asking for opioids, for God's sake."

Use of the phone, however, was beyond Bud's capabilities. Summoning all the restraint I could muster, I decided not to throttle him, which I really wanted to do, but instead chose to never patronize this pharmacy again and to engage in a phone campaign to get this guy fired. Unfortunately, when he ultimately was fired, he naturally turned up at the only other major pharmacy in town, requiring me to switch back to the pharmacy that I had originally boycotted to avoid him.

I'm not sure who won this standoff, but I am happy to report that I suffered only these two instances of insensitive behavior during my cancer treatment. I would venture to guess that two episodes of bad behavior over the scope of six months is far below the average experienced by most people over the same time frame. The negative encounters that I experienced were far overshadowed by the family members, friends, nurses, physicians, strangers, and acquaintances who went out of their way to be helpful. As far as I'm concerned, those are pretty good odds.

PART SEVEN:

The Recovery

CHAPTER 24

LET *Your* FREAK FLAG FLY

Long, Beautiful Hair

A few weeks after I completed radiation, my hair started to grow back. Because of my pixie-cut childhood trauma, I have never been happy with short hair. Now, however, the concept of a bad hair day had new meaning. I started with teeny gray curly hair and thought it was pretty cool. Then, I noticed that I looked startlingly like my mom. Mom is beautiful, but by definition she is older than I am, and I don't know too many women who are trying to look older, so I was not that interested in sporting the Mom look for too long.

Me looking like Mom   Actual Mom

Once again, out of blissful ignorance, I decided I might as well dye my hair red, since it was short anyway, and I had nothing to lose. I found out after the fact that you're not supposed to dye your hair right away after chemo. Don't know why, because it didn't seem to do me any harm, but that's what I was told.

After this whole cancer experience, I was ready to try a few things way outside of my usual comfort zone. My sister, Laura, sagely advised me on this topic: "Let your freak flag fly!" So, Bob and I went out to the garage with the messiest batch of organic henna ever and dyed my hair red, not auburn this time but flaming red. After a couple of weeks, I decided that my new look could only be improved by a gray streak in the front. I referred to this streak, depending on my mood, as my Bonnie Raitt or Bride-of-Frankenstein streak.

Bob with "Janis"

I'm now happy to report that Janis is back! Two years after my hair started to grow back in, I look like myself again. When I walk out in the fog and it does its thing, I am proud. I had my first post-treatment keratin session a couple of months ago and am once again in love with my Pantene hair.

Exercise

The cancer literature, which I finally read just last week, says that exercise decreases fatigue and helps you sleep better. It can also improve your quality of life and emotional well-being and reduce stress and appetite loss. Yoga, Tai Chi, meditation, and guided imagery are offered at many cancer treatment facilities and were offered to me when I was a patient at the cancer spa.

During my treatment, staying in shape did mean a lot to my outlook and well-being. I was not trying to set any new records in my level of fitness. I just wanted to maintain my current weight and shape as much as I could. Although there were days where my exercise consisted of lifting the remote to find a new Netflix series to binge-watch (*Nurse Jackie* is great when you're feeling under the weather), I found that I could typically do more than I expected.

My community offered a variety of fitness classes designed to avoid putting undue stress on aging bones. This was a perfect way to keep up my strength and stay in shape during my cancer treatment, so I happily wandered over to the gym for classes almost every day with my little scarf-thing on my head. Wearing a wig while exercising is a bad idea. It could slip around and is way too hot. I met a great friend at these classes, Sharon, and often it was only the two of us. Taking advantage of the situation, we would plead with the instructors: "Your job is to keep us out of the nursing home. We're freaking old, and we need strength and balance." They agreed that both were necessary—weights and weight-bearing activities to stave off bone density loss and balance to keep us from falling over and breaking a hip. Thus, the focus of each class became strength and balance.

Sharon, who is a few years older than I am, started working out at age sixty and now goes to Body Pump on a regular basis. She is an awesome role model. After my cancer treatment was complete and I was determined to get back to my former level of fitness, I went to Body Pump with her once and found it to be a combination of weight lifting and aerobics. Sharon led me to the weight room and loaded up a bar with about twenty pounds of weights on either end for herself. Since I was new, I figured I could only handle about ten pounds of weights. Five minutes into the class, I had to take all the weights off my bar. By the end of the class, I had dropped the bar altogether. And that was my last experience with Body Pump.

I went skiing whenever possible, though. That was why we had moved to the mountains, right? I always feel as if I am in college again whenever I ski. I can go as fast as I want, providing my own cheap thrills. The ski resort is only ten minutes away from our house. It is very easy to hop on the shuttle to the mountain and get in a couple hours of skiing on any given weekday. When we lived in the Bay Area and came up for the weekend, we always thought we had to ski each day until we dropped, just to get our money's worth and to justify the long drive and the hassle of packing food, kids, and clothes for the weekend. Living next to the resort, it's a great afternoon break. I can work all morning, then have a pretend "meeting" or a series of "conference calls" during the afternoon, head back to the "office" by 4:30, and return calls or tend to any other business to wrap up the day. Yes, I still have fake meetings and conference calls.

I soon discovered that no one could tell that I was going through chemo once I put my ski helmet on! One day, Bob and I were out skiing. It was perfect weather, crystal clear, and the views were stunning. Bob and I were taking pictures of each other with the lake view from the top of the mountain, and I felt great. I was hamming it up for the

The back of the infamous
FML T-shirt

camera and raised my ski poles for no particular reason. When I sent the photo to my mom and sister, they cried. They interpreted the photo as a victory salute toward the end of my cancer treatment. Maybe it was. This photo now graces the back of the FML T-shirt but has been modified so that I am holding several trophies.

The last lap in my victory salute was wakeboarding. Bob and I now take an annual trip up to Huntington Lake with friends, the same people we were meeting up with after the wig-shopping expedition toward the beginning of my cancer treatment. Our friends only had one women's wetsuit, which we shared. Initially, we didn't know each other all that well, and Carol always

Me, alive!

politely let me ski first in a dry, warm wetsuit. Once we got to know each other, however, it became a standoff for who would go first. If you've ever tried to wriggle into a cold, wet wetsuit, you know how uncomfortable and challenging that can be. I temporarily regained the honors for the dry wetsuit the year I had cancer, so I jumped at the opportunity to wakeboard and had a blast. Red curly locks blowing in the wind, cold water, fresh air. I was alive!

It Was a Dark 'n' Stormy Night

Vacation is another critical ingredient in feeling better. The Christmas after my last cancer treatment, my family and I headed to the British Virgin Islands to charter a sailboat and go sailing for a week. We brought along Kelly's boyfriend Chad for the ride. This was one of my favorite trips of all time. My family was packed into a few square feet for a full week. Since my girls were now both in college, it was a rare opportunity to get to know them as adults.

There were great and funny moments during this particular trip. One of my favorite memories was when Chad stuck his head out of the cabin and yelled, "Papa Croshaw, is there supposed to be this much smoke down here?" We were just approaching a tight passage where we were relying on the engine to get us through in control, preferably without bumping up against some rocks.

Well, you don't need to be a seasoned mariner to know that smoke billowing out of the cabin is probably not a good thing. I was well on my way to jumping off the boat and swimming for safety when I took stock of my parental obligations and decided to stick it out on board. Bob was at the wheel, and I was with him in the cockpit. He rushed to the engine compartment and grabbed the fire extinguisher. He was just about to activate the extinguisher when he decided to check the engine belts first.

It turned out the smoke was from the coolant, billowing out of the engine compartment from a broken belt hitting the overheated engine. Fortunately, we were able to contact the charter company, who sent a guy out to replace the belt. Within an hour or two, we were on our way. Over some "dark 'n' stormies," a delicious sailing drink made from rum and ginger beer, that night we had lots of giggles and guffaws over the incident. Looking back, it could have gotten ugly, but it didn't, and we were all feeling pretty grateful that we got through it without too much inconvenience.

My best memory from the trip happened on Christmas Day. We arrived at the Baths in Virgin Gorda, truly one of the most beautiful beaches in the world. To access the beach by sailboat, you have to bring the dinghy to one beach, then hike through a series of caves to another beach (the Baths), which is surrounded by huge boulders. It was a perfect day. The

Christmas at the Baths, en famille

water was eighty-plus degrees, and the air temperature was about the same. We splashed and swam in the water for hours. Before we left, we took this Christmas photo. I'm the one in the funky scarf-hat thing, obviously!

If you catch me in a weak moment, this photo can bring tears to my eyes. While I generally shy away from standing next to my daughters in bikinis, I was feeling good enough to take a chance on that *and* be photographed in the scarf-hat thing. I will admit that, while the photo was taken, I was sucking it in to the best of my ability and didn't take a breath until I got the all clear that the photo was good. But the photo wasn't all about me. I believe it shows that all of us had gotten through cancer and were back to focusing on fun adventures.

LIFE *After* CANCER— FML, *the* SEQUEL

FOR THOSE OF YOU WHO have never had cancer, the treatment isn't really over when you walk out the door after radiation, despite the hokey bell-ringing tradition. There are a gazillion follow-up appointments, tests (mammograms, bone density, blood draws), and in my case, hormone therapy. Since my cancer was hormone responsive, I was prescribed Arimidex, an aromatase inhibitor, which blocks estrogen from being produced in postmenopausal women. Initially, I was to take this drug for ten years after the conclusion of my treatment, but there is now discussion in the medical community about reducing that time frame to five years in some cases. So far, I have no idea whether I will fall into the five-year category. Immediately I was miserable taking this drug, so I tried one or two other alternatives. The alternatives were no better, so I went back to Arimidex, which is considered more beneficial than the others.

Arimidex is supposed to reduce the chance of a recurrence, but this drug is no picnic. Imagine going through menopause, getting fairly close to the end of the hot-flash phase, then re-embarking on that phase for another ten years. This is one of the reasons that I love living in a place where it snows. Frequently during the winter, I will get up from watching TV and go out to stand in the snow for a few minutes while my body temperature comes back to normal. If I didn't do this, I would be concerned that our sofa would spontaneously combust from the heat that my body generates. I've also been known to leave the dinner table for the same purpose. Nobody seems to mind, and it works! That is my reality. But as they say about getting older, it sure beats the alternative.

One Step Forward, Two Steps Back

Well on my way to recovery, my current oncologist, Nancy, reminded me to follow up on that nagging thyroid lump she had noticed during one of her exams. I had already been to a surgeon about this at the very beginning of my cancer treatment, and he assured me it was nothing. Now, however, Nancy thought I should go to the endocrinology experts at the University of California, San Francisco (UCSF) and explore this further. I'd had enough medical appointments to last me a lifetime, so I was not anxious to follow up on anything for which I had already been cleared. It was only to humor her—and very reluctantly—that I did.

On my next trip to San Francisco, I made an appointment at the endocrinology clinic at UCSF. Once again, in the doctor's office, we went through the exam and the ridiculously long ultrasound. The radiologist started to say, "Hmm, this is concerning . . ." By now I know that "concerning" translates to "you have cancer." It turns out I had papillary thyroid carcinoma on both sides of my thyroid gland, requiring a complete removal of my thyroid. I should stress that this was not an instance where breast cancer had metastasized to another organ but a concurrence of two separate and distinct cancers.

I did learn from the endocrine surgeon that he had seen thyroid cancer and breast cancer concurrently more than once, and he believed there was some connection. Of course, I did enough Internet research to corroborate his comments. I found that "the development of both breast and thyroid cancer has been shown to be affected by hormonal risk factors. [. . .] Evidence suggests that the increased risk for subsequent thyroid cancer seen among breast-cancer survivors is specific for papillary thyroid cancer,[1]" which is what I had. Healthline.com reports that a history of breast cancer increases your risk of thyroid cancer and vice versa. So, it turns out the follow-up on thyroid cancer at the insistence of my oncologist was not simply a wild goose chase. Women with either thyroid or breast cancer should be aware of the risk that one can be associated with the other.

In any event, thyroid surgery is relatively painless and has a quick recovery. The surgeons try to position the incision at a place where you already have creases (i.e., wrinkles) in your neck so the scar is not tremendously obvious. Since Laura has also had thyroid issues, I don't think I was even in the running for the FML prize that week. The lingering consequences are that I will be on Synthroid for the rest of my life with even more follow-up testing, ultrasounds, and appointments. I can deal with that.

* * *

During the active-treatment phase of my cancer, I never realized that my cancer being HR positive would turn out to be the biggest nightmare of my entire cancer treatment experience. It led to adjutant hormone therapy after the other treatments were complete, which entailed taking an estrogen-blocking hormone for five to ten years after chemo and radiation. A complete lack of estrogen can have severe consequences, and in my case it did.

The first issue I experienced was a chronic urinary tract infection (UTI). I went through multiple courses of antibiotics, but they didn't seem to be working. It wasn't a severe, acute condition, just a nagging one. One day, after this had already gone on for months, I was driving to the Bay Area for work. About an hour from home, I lost the ability to tell left from right and couldn't figure out what the GPS was telling me to do. *Why is that woman yelling at me?* I thought. Meanwhile, I was rerouted several times, unable to understand her directions. I thought possibly that my confusion was a consequence of forgetting to take my thyroid medicine for a few days, so I searched for a pharmacy, finding that they were all closed at this hour.

I finally ended up at a restaurant, trying to sort out what was happening. When seated in the back of the restaurant, I requested that the hostess move me to the front, where she could keep an eye on me. I ordered dinner and a beer, certain that a tiny bit of alcohol might calm me down as I pondered my next move. I knew I would be in the restaurant for a while, so I brought in a box of photos from my car. I was sorting out all the family photos to scan them so that they would be in a format that my children would be able to access in the future. I stared at the pictures of the kids in school, on vacation, and doing various sports. I was unable to understand any of these activities as categories, so frankly, I couldn't sort a single photo. Around this time, the manager stopped by my booth to ask if I needed anything. My speech was as jumbled as my thoughts. He asked if he should call 911, and realizing how my confusion had completely taken over, I said yes.

A few minutes later, an attractive young ambulance crew arrived. Immediately, they snatched away my beer. I was lucid enough to understand that that was probably a good move. They asked me a few questions, then took me by ambulance to the hospital, where I was diagnosed with delirium from a chronic UTI. It's something that usually only happens to women in their eighties or nineties, so I felt "special" to be having the experience in my sixties. I was given massive doses of antibiotics and was fine the next day. When I saw a urologist later to treat the ongoing infections, he advised me that it was a side effect of the estrogen-blocking hormone. I was prescribed a low dose of antibiotics for a year after that, and the UTIs now seem to be under control.

Another side effect was considerably more serious. I have a strong family history of bipolar disorder and was, therefore, pre-disposed to it. I had experienced depressive moments previously in my life but never a manic episode, which is the defining diagnostic criteria for bipolar disorder. Depression alone is described as uni-polar. Unfortunately, as I was told, the estrogen blocker was likely a factor in unleashing this potential in a dramatic and life-changing way, leading to a severe manic phase, during which I didn't sleep for days on end and set out to "conquer the world." I stayed up all night, reading, writing, watching TV, and playing games on my phone. I tried breathing exercises guided by my Apple Watch in a vain attempt to induce sleep but gave up after half an hour or so. My mind was racing too quickly to concentrate on one thing, like breathing. I also experienced one of my most fiscally damaging shopping sprees. I went into a high-end boutique and bought the most expensive accessories that I could find. My logic was that if I had these key items, they would last forever. It made perfect sense to me but not to my budget.

As things progressed, I became ultra-sensitive to sounds, par-ticularly human voices. In the car, I couldn't listen to any music with words. Then I became unable to stand the sound of any music at all. A human voice was like nails on a chalkboard, so I asked everyone around me to just be silent. Then, I started to scream—at everyone, including my immediate family and strangers. At one point, I created a scene in a Starbucks, and the cops were called. My sister and her husband were with me and assured the cops that they were taking me to get help. In short, I was off the rails. Bipolar disorder is something that is normally diagnosed when people are in their twenties, and almost never in their sixties. Again, I felt special in all the wrong ways.

Consistent with the theme that every action causes an equal and opposite reaction, depressive episodes immediately followed the manic episode. I went through intense treatment for most of a summer. The treatment left me unable to work, travel, or even talk on the phone. If I was interrupted, I lost my train of thought irretrievably and became quite frustrated. Math and logic became another source of frustration for me. The psychiatrist who helped me through this time believed that the estrogen blocker at least contributed to and may have even triggered the severe manic episode. I had difficulty accepting this idea, so I came back and asked her, "How sure are you that the estrogen blocker contributed?"

"One hundred percent," she answered.

Still wondering about this conclusion, I again resorted to the Internet, where I discovered chat rooms and a series of scientific articles addressing this issue, all of which convinced me that her theory was correct. One study at Oxford concluded that "caution may be warranted when employing aromatase inhibitors, especially in women with a past history of postpartum affective disorder or bipolar disorder. [. . .] The primary mechanism of the effect may be acute reduction in circulating estrogen levels."[2] I would add to the list of situations to be treated with caution "women with a family history of bipolar disorder," just to be safe. Another article reported that "mood disturbances, somnolence, anxiety, fatigue, hot flashes, and memory impairment have been reported among patients receiving Anastrazole (also known as Arimidex) as adjuvant therapy."[3] That conclusion was based on the case of a fifty-six-year-old woman with no prior psychiatric history who was diagnosed with hormone-receptor-positive early-stage breast cancer (as I was) and who developed severe mood changes after administration of Anastrozole, which resolved after discontinuation of treatment.[4] Bipolar disorder is an extreme "mood disturbance." Unfortunately, once those mood changes have progressed to bipolar disorder, the mood changes can no longer be reversed. What I also discovered during my research is that another aromatase inhibitor, Tamoxifen, is actually believed to decrease manic symptoms associated with bipolar disorder and "shows potential as a treatment for episodes of mania in patients with bipolar disorder."[5]

At my next follow-up meeting with my oncologist, I asked her whether she had any experience with Anastrozole causing or contributing to bipolar disorder. It was a rare enough phenomenon that she had never seen it happen in her entire experience as an oncologist. She immediately offered to change or discontinue the hormone therapy, but it was too late. Most women going through hormone therapy after breast cancer will not experience these side effects, but I was in a unique category of women who did. This latest ordeal earned me, once again, the lifetime achievement title in the FML contest with my sister, who insisted I hold on to the T-shirt a little longer. I was in no position to argue.

Cancer TAKEAWAYS

WHEN I BECAME PREGNANT FOR the first time, I had an overwhelming feeling that I had finally joined the human experience. People I had never met stopped me on the streets to congratulate me. Mothers from every background offered to share stories. Men and women alike treated me with kindness. I had an epiphany that until that time, I had lived my life in a bubble, with most human activity circling around me without actually *touching* me. Having a child brought me the opportunity to share experiences with others whom I may never have met and opened my world beyond my imagination. Cancer is the other experience in my life that left me with the same feeling. Cancer connects you to everyone who has ever had cancer, everyone who has ever had a friend or loved one with cancer, medical professionals who treat cancer, and even those who have experienced any kind of medical trauma in the course of their lives.

One of my takeaways from having had cancer is that I became somewhat offended by the idea that survivors were brave and had "fought" cancer. In my mind, this is a qualitative comment about things people have no control over. It's not a fight—it's a circumstance. It's a circumstance that sucks to varying degrees. I never want to pass judgment on the person who died from cancer or who suffered more than I did on the premise that they didn't fight hard enough. Cancer is not about aggression or competition, which I relate to fighting.

Another conclusion that should be obvious, but isn't, is that people (including cancer patients) should not be put in the position of cheering *you* up if they are having a bad day. For this reason I have never condoned asking someone, especially a stranger, to "smile!" if they're not feeling up to it, but I do believe that the whole cancer experience can be improved by trying to look on the bright side and, yes, even smiling when the situation warrants.

At the end of my treatment, the staff at the cancer center asked if I would fill out a form for a staff member or medical professional who went above and beyond. I couldn't bring myself to do it. Every person I had encountered at the center was truly amazing, all in different ways. Maybe their inherent humanity was what led them to the career path that they chose. In retrospect, I realize that I could have just said that on the form, but I wasn't thinking. I hope if the doctors, nurses, and staff at the cancer center read the dedication to this book, it will be a sufficient enough gesture to help them understand how much they contribute to a patient's well-being during a difficult time, as well as how much it is appreciated by the patients.

And I can't sign off without mentioning that Bob chose to take one for the team during my treatment, as far as our family was concerned. Our daughters were understandably concerned about my cancer, so, for several months, he did not even mention to them that he had been diagnosed with prostate cancer at about the same time I was diagnosed with breast cancer. He didn't think it was fair for them to be concerned about *both* of their parents at once. That was the real reason behind our couples' tour of the cancer center upon our arrival in Truckee.

Around the time I had my thyroidectomy, Bob was undergoing radiation for prostate cancer. Not ideal family time, but we got to share stories about the staff and swap radiation experiences. And yes, I actually earned two massages per week at the cancer center, one as a patient and one as a caregiver. I am happy to say that we are both doing well, and we are planning to keep on smilin' through whatever rain comes our way. We are now filling our time with sailing and other adventures and hoping the cancer center can do without us for a while.

ACKNOWLEDGMENTS

AS WITH ALL ACKNOWLEDGMENTS, THERE are too many people who have helped get me this far, and I don't want to offend a single one by the order in which they are mentioned. So, maybe alphabetically would work best. But even with that equalizing approach, family has to come first.

I'd like to start with my husband, Bob. Not only did he offer me encouragement in writing this book at a time when I had never written anything other than legal documents, but he was also there to offer his support in all the ugly moments and to share in the good moments when we were fortunate enough to have them. And, in spite of my hair fixation, my appearance was never an issue for him. I could wear a wig or not around the house, and he was fine with it either way. I also want to thank him for helping me dye my hair when it started to grow back in. This was not an easy task for him, but we turned my gray hair into a lovely flaming red when I was ready to try something different. Bob has never even liked red hair, but we were both pleased with the results.

As an engineer with no literary background, he turned out to be surprisingly helpful in the development of the book. He read every sentence each time I finished a draft and pointed out sections that needed explanation. He also corrected inconsistencies and sometimes even grammar. Unfortunately, we shared the cancer experience more than we wanted to, since he was going through cancer treatments at the same time I was, but I have to think that it made each of us more understanding of what the other was experiencing.

Next, of course, are my daughters, Kelly and Ren. Kelly offered to go to Croatia with Bob at a time when I couldn't go. I know this doesn't sound like a huge sacrifice, but it encouraged Bob to do something he had looked forward to for years, and it gave me the time alone that I needed. After the trip, when she was back at school, she often called to check in and see how things were going. Anyone with college-age children knows that these calls are to be treasured. She cheered me on, banned me from the kitchen on Thanksgiving, and wrote an incredible tribute on Instagram, saying I was one of the strongest people that she knew. Cancer didn't cause me to cry much, but that tribute sure did.

My daughter Ren's caring and nourishing character was a tremendous support throughout my treatment. Ren has a thousand things going on in her life, most of which involve helping others. She has helped the homeless, spent New Year's Eve with AIDS patients, and helped countless people through body therapy, yoga, and nutrition. She was in school at the time my illness hit. When she took time out from her activities to cook for me and just spend time with me, I felt deeply touched and somewhat selfish for taking her time from others. She also kicked me out of the kitchen on Thanksgiving, and I will forever be grateful to both of my daughters for doing that.

My sister, Laura, contributed inspirationally and acted as my editor in the early stages of this book. She offered blunt and honest feedback, which is the only kind that's worth anything. I still hope we can go on *Oprah* together, because without her encouragement, this book would not exist. At one point, when I texted her and said, "I think my book is crap. Am I wasting my time?" she responded with what she called the four phases of any creative process, which went something like this: 1) My book is crap. 2) I am crap. 3) Hmm, maybe there's something here. And 4) I kinda like this. I was clearly in phase 1, but I was encouraged to learn that others had the same thoughts during the creative process.

Laura also supported me through my treatment. She and her family came to visit, with their dog, Sunny, of course. We never really talked about cancer much, but we cracked ourselves up over other things, which was far more important. She even went so far as to offer up Sunny as a temporary emotional support animal, and Sunny happily rose to the occasion. The only mention of cancer that I recall from her visit was when we were waiting to be seated at a restaurant. We had waited a while, and I wasn't feeling strong enough to stand up for more than a few minutes, so I told Laura that if they didn't seat us in five minutes, I was going to rip my wig off and see if that got things moving. We almost fell over laughing, but luckily, we were seated within the five minutes, so I didn't have to follow through on the threat.

Then comes Mom, or Big M, as Laura and I refer to her. The nickname came about because she has a personality that can fill a room, even though she is five foot nothing and has always claimed to be five foot two. Big M was always available to chat by phone, usually railing about the political events of the day. She was a great distraction from the issues at hand. When she came to visit, she did everything she could to help, despite the fact that she had fallen down the stairs of the airplane and suffered an ankle injury on her way. She, too, was a party to the conspiracy to ban me from the kitchen on Thanksgiving. She knew at that point, that crying and pity weren't really going to lift my spirits, so if she did engage in those activities (which I assume she did), she took great care not to do them in my presence. Thanks for that, Big M!

Of course, I want to thank my editor, Diana Ceres. Yes, I know I have now departed from alphabetical order, but I'm done with family now. Choosing an editor for a first book is a daunting task, so I interviewed many candidates. In the same way that teachers say that the A-paper floats to the top, Diana's qualifications and personality floated to the top of my list. We immediately seemed to click, and she knew exactly how to coach me to fill in areas where the reader may have been lost. I have no doubt that this book is an infinitely better product because of her efforts.

Another group, out of order, is my "beta group," that group of close friends who agreed to read an early version of the book and to give me their feedback. In a variety of ways, they encouraged me to move forward with the book, even when I was in that self-deprecatory phase of the creative process. I thank each one for their thoughts, comments, suggestions, and most of all, friendship.

And last, but absolutely not least, I want to thank Jenny. Her friendship over the years and through different circumstances meant a lot to me even before the events of this book took place. She was an outspoken friend who pushed me to do the right thing at the right time. I can't think of another person in my life who could have convinced me to take time out of my busy schedule, when I was working full time and moving, for my life-changing 3-D mammogram at the Women's Center before moving to Tahoe. She used the right combination of persuasion and insistence to spur me to action. I only hope that those of you reading this book have a friend like Jenny, or that perhaps you are that friend.

ABOUT *the* AUTHOR

CATHY CROSHAW AND HER HUSBAND, Bob, are both native Californians. They met while skiing in Squaw Valley, got married, and raised two girls. Cathy practiced law in San Francisco for thirty-seven years and retired in the summer of 2018. Bob worked in the electronics industry with his most recent job as CEO of an electronics distribution company.

They now live near Lake Tahoe and spend several weeks of the year chartering sailboats around the world, combined with some land travel. When they're not traveling, they take advantage of Truckee's snowy winters for skiing and its warm summers for hiking with their dog, Charlie. They also enjoy playing golf and spending time at the lake.

In 2014, both Cathy and Bob had cancer and were treated at the Gene Upshaw Memorial Cancer Center in Truckee. Today, Cathy keeps a blog of their travels and is also writing articles about their unique experiences sailing in various parts of the world. To learn more about the author and her latest adventures, visit www.cathycroshaw.com.

ENDNOTES

Chapter 25

1. Nielsen, S. et al. "The Breast-Thyroid Cancer Link: A Systematic Review and Meta-analysis." *Cancer Epidemiology Biomarkers & Prevention*, February 2016, Volume 25, Issue 2: 231–238. DOI: 10.1158/1055-9965.EPI-15-0833.

2. Goodwin, G. M. "Aromatase Inhibitors and Bipolar Mood Disorder: A Case Report." *Bipolar Disorders*, October 16, 2006, Volume 8, Issue 5p1: 516–518. DOI: 10.1111/j.1399-5618.2006.00367.

3. Rocha-Cadman, X., M. J. Massie, K. Du Hamel. "Aromatase Inhibitors and Mood Disturbances." *Palliative & Supportive Care*, September 2012, Volume 10, Issue 3: 225–227. DOI: 10.1017/S1478951512000636.

4. Ibid.

5. Palacios, J. et al. "Tamoxifen for Bipolar Disorder: Systematic Review and Meta-analysis." *Journal of Psychopharmacology*, February 11, 2019, Volume 33, Issue 2: 177–184. DOI:10.1177/0269881118822167.

Made in the USA
Coppell, TX
01 August 2020